Intentional Leader

Your leaders. Our passion.

Copyright © 2020 by Revela

ISBN: 9798662687011
Ebook ASIN: B08CJ6W3RL
Independently Published

All rights reserved. No part of this book may be reproduced or transmitted in any form, by any means, electronic or mechanical, including photocopying, recording, or by any information storage and retrieval system, without permission in writing from the copyright owner. For more information on distribution rights, royalties, derivative works, or licensing opportunities on behalf of this content or work, please contact the publisher at the address below.

Printed in the United States of America.

Secondary Author: Andrea Fredrickson
Cover Design: Ashta Johnson

Although the author and publisher have made every effort to ensure that the information and advice in this book was correct and accurate at press time, the author and publisher do not assume and hereby disclaim any liability to any party for any loss, damage, or disruption caused from acting upon the information in this book or by errors or omissions, whether such errors or omissions results from negligence, accident, or any other cause.

Revela
1508 Leavenworth Street
Omaha, NE 68102
RevelaGroup.com

Table of Contents

Foreword 1
Introduction 3
Chapter 1: Basic Communication 14
Chapter 2: The Cost of Keeping Score 31
Chapter 3: Crucial Conversations 51
Chapter 4: Make Time to Manage Time 71
Chapter 5: Opportunities to Lead 92
Chapter 6: Making Things Better 111
About Revela 130
References 132

Foreword

Every day, in companies throughout the world, people are working hard and doing their best to provide value to their companies and customers. They are provided with a job description, outlining the scope of their responsibilities. Next, they're oriented to the company, and provided a few weeks of training to get up to speed. Some will find friendly co-workers who will help them navigate the ins and outs of "how things are done around here," but most of the training is technical in nature. All important stuff!

Companies want people to be leaders; people who provide value to the company and their customers. The question that is at the base of this desire is, "How?" Learning to be a leader and to provide value requires a mindset that is intentional about serving others.

Some people are fortunate to have had others in their lives that are great models of leadership, and they work hard to exemplify those behaviors: finding ways to lift people up, make things better, communicate with intention and heart, and otherwise be of service. Yet even for those who have great role models, they may need reminders, or they may need to be challenged to build their leadership skills. It doesn't make a difference if you hold a position of leadership or not; everyone benefits from developing leadership skills.

What if employees were given tools, resources, training, and feedback on how to be more effective early in their career or new role? What if they were taught how to practice and hone these skills so that everyone understood how to provide value for the company and its customers?

This book, along with other books by Revela, has been written to provide companies with a way to do just that for their employees. It can be read as a standalone guide, or it can be used in one of the many programs offered by Revela. Using research and processes to help people get information into their long-term memory, employees are then able to pull that information when they need it, and not just to pass a test.

Leading takes practice. Just like learning the skills that create expert technicians, leaders must be given what it takes to be successful. And then they must intentionally sharpen those new skills so they can be experts in their role.

At Revela, we believe employees, those who manage and lead others and those who don't, have the right to be successful. Companies need the best resources to help them. We're here to help.

Introduction

What's the Next Step in Your Career?

You can make good things happen...

Have you ever stopped to think about how you got here? What led to this point in your career? Did you get here by accident, or was it intentional? What and who influenced you along the way? And who have you influenced?

Think back to the people and events that led you to your current position at work. You probably remember a time when you asked for a specific job. You may have been inspired to learn new things or were influenced in other ways by your colleagues or supervisors. Maybe there were times you were just in the right place at the right time. Can you think of a day when you persuaded your boss to let you work on a special project or used your personal influence to help coworkers sort out an agreement?

Decisions, events, and interactions like these are the work of leaders. You might not think of yourself as a leader, but whenever you acted with intention and inspired or influenced others, you were being a leader. Anyone who has a vision of something and works with others to reach that vision – that person is a leader.

Everyone is a leader within some aspect of their lives. In the workplace, organizations often look for people who show specific leadership qualities. It sets them apart.

Think about the attitudes of people you know at work.
Some people go to work because it's just what they do. They know work is a necessity for living life and providing for a family. These people go to work simply to get a paycheck and put food on the table. It really doesn't matter to them what job they have, as long as it pays the bills. This type of person often simply allows things to happen at home and at work.

Other people want more. They want a challenge. Opportunities to learn. New experiences. They know they need money to sustain life, but there's something else they look forward to every day when they go to work. They want their mind to be stimulated. They look forward to encouragement from others to help them be better at what they do. These people also love to help others. They enjoy having an important role and contributing to something bigger than themselves. They want to make things happen.

The second type of person is usually very intentional when they choose a job. They see each position as a steppingstone in building their career. Not only that, they want to work for a company they can be proud of – a company that provides them with opportunities to do meaningful work; to make a difference and keep on learning.

Maybe you haven't thought you were being intentional in the building of your career. But being a leader doesn't always mean moving "up the ladder." You can stay in the same position and build your career simply by growing your knowledge and experience right where you are. You can be intentional about it and use your influence to help people around you. "Growing in place" can be just as good for your career as climbing the ladder, and it's also valuable for your organization.

Are You a Leader?

When you think of the word "leader," what comes to mind? There are leaders of European countries, leaders of rock bands, and leaders in car races. For many people, the word "leader" brings up images of people in management or company owners. True, many managers have leadership titles, but being a leader isn't really about a title or position. It's about behaving like a leader. It's a mindset of getting things done and helping other people succeed.

Here are a few of the many actions that demonstrate leadership:
- Showing empathy
- Communicating effectively
- Influencing others positively
- Following through
- Being honest
- Having a positive attitude
- Serving others
- Acting consistently

Some characteristics are common to all effective leaders. One of the most important is the ability to influence people. Influence is the power to change or affect someone or something – the power to cause changes without directly forcing them to happen. We can influence others just by our presence.

Consider What People Think of You

Everything you do communicates something. You can't not communicate. As you sit here reading this book, you are communicating to those around you. If others look at you while you read, they are receiving a message about you.

There are many things you do that communicate to others, influencing their opinion of you. How you dress, your appearance, and how you carry yourself. Do you have manners and use proper etiquette? Do you act with integrity? Are you honest? What are the values that guide your life, and are your actions congruent with them? Do you recognize your strengths and weaknesses? How are you managing your weaknesses to align with your values? Do you demonstrate courage, make decisions, and learn from your mistakes? Consider what people think of you. Do they see you as a person who cares about people and thinks the best of them? Do your colleagues see you thinking ahead, communicating effectively, and following through? Would they consider you the type of person who is a leader? Take a moment to think about this. Then, decide whether you believe your behaviors reflect the way you want to be perceived by others.

It's All About Choices

Practically every action we take is the result of a choice. You chose to go to work today. A stop sign on the way to work demanded that you stop, and you chose to obey it. Are you reading this page by choice? Of course, all of those things are choices. You might not like the consequences of not going to work or not stopping at a stop sign, but they are choices. Even deciding not to make a choice...is a choice!

Making choices and moving ahead based on what you believe will happen is what we call "being intentional." According to

Merriam-Webster, intention means "the thing you plan to do or achieve: an aim or purpose." You chose to read this book, because it is your intention to develop your leadership skills. In other words, becoming a better leader is your goal. You've already started! Just thinking about developing your leadership skills is taking a step in that direction.

Throughout the book, we will discuss ways you can become more intentional about this goal. You'll learn how to demonstrate specific leadership behaviors and we'll provide techniques to help you hone the skills you already have, so you can make a difference and be the effective leader you want to be.

Leaders as Effective Team Members

Here's an interesting fact about leaders: the qualities that make them good leaders also make them very effective team members. In this book, you'll learn how to use your leadership qualities to be a more effective team member.

For example, with your leadership qualities you can inspire your teammates. You can encourage them to take responsibility, to communicate, and to collaborate in effective ways. You'll learn how your personal style and approach to communication and collaboration impacts the outcome. We'll help you discover ways to make slight adjustments in your interactions with others. This will improve your ability to collaborate with and influence those around you, so you can work together toward mutual goals

The learning process will encourage you to share your goals, ask questions, and learn from other people's perspectives and experiences. We suggest allowing yourself to engage fully in the process. Start this process wholeheartedly!

By the time you are finished with the book, you will have a strong new set of skills and resources you can draw on any time. You will have taken one big leap ahead toward a future full of successful achievements as an effective leader and valuable team member.

Characteristics of a Good Team Member

The chapters in this book are full of practical ideas and encouraging advice about using your leadership and team member skills to make things happen. You'll learn how to cultivate useful skills you already have. And you'll acquire some new skills.

Effective team members use the same qualities to influence people and outcomes that effective leaders use:

Good Communicators

Who, on your team, do you think of as highly successful? Those team members likely are effective communicators, and realize they must consciously adjust their communication style to the person they're talking to if they want to be understood. They take responsibility for making sure their messages are understood as intended. Good communicators understand that miscommunications happen, and that it doesn't help to place blame.

Professional

When situations become difficult or are emotionally-charged, a professional leader or team member is able to intentionally remain calm. This involves carrying oneself in a professional manner and behaving respectfully toward others, with comments that appear to be intentional and thought-out. Even the emails of a professional are easy to read and understand. These team members follow professional guidelines, successfully balancing a personal touch with professional boundaries.

Motivated

Motivated and inspired workers are productive and committed to the organization. They are not only personally motivated, but they help others work to their fullest potential. They are not concerned only about their own success, but about the success of others and the organization. They take time to understand what's good for others, themselves, and the business. They know how to create win-win situations.

Assume Positive Intent

In this book, you'll be challenged to develop a belief that the intentions of others are generally positive. We will show you how others are just like you. They come to work intending to do the right thing, with a desire to be a valuable contributor to the organization. Seeing people's good intentions requires a certain attitude. It requires being receptive to and enthusiastic about the ideas and perspectives of others. When you assume positive intent, you invite your colleagues to participate in the conversation, and you encourage shared ownership in processes and projects.

Continuous Learner

Just think how much has changed since you began your career. Do you complete work a different way now than you did when you started? Maybe you've learned new ways of thinking and communicating to stay on top of new technology or find a solution to a complex problem. Businesses continually look for ways to develop new efficiencies and improve quality. They need people who are open to exploring new ideas and learning new ways to do business.

All of these qualities are tools successful team members – and leaders – use to influence outcomes. These qualities must be nurtured in order to grow. We want to help you do that.

Some people believe continuous learning is the most important of these skills. Your organization relies on you to look down the road and stay on top of business and industry trends. They expect you to learn and share new ideas. They need your perspective to improve operations and make the organization's success more likely. How can you influence anyone, change a bad situation, or find new ways of doing things if you don't have the proper background information? It's up to you to make continuous learning a part of who you are and what you do.

True, learning can be a challenge in today's environment. The pace of innovation is fast. Information is flooding into the workplace. How is it possible to absorb so much in so little time? The thought of learning in this environment can be intimidating. Here are a few tips for learning that apply to this program or any other learning opportunity:

See, Hear, and Do.
Anyone is far more likely to retain information when they are exposed to it at least three times in three different ways: when they see it, hear it, and apply it. Throughout this book, we ask that you first read the material in each chapter, then listen to it several times using the audio version. And finally, practice. Put into action the things you've learned.

Purposeful Practice.
Thousands of hours of practice and training are required to stage successful professional dance and music performances. Likewise, no one becomes a virtuoso leader or team member without practicing communication skills over and over. The

actionable pieces of information in this book provide a fabulous opportunity for practice. Take advantage of these opportunities to try out new approaches.

Repeat.
To lock in your new skills, keep absorbing related information. Look for opportunities to see, hear, and test your skills. Practice them until they become habits. Be determined to soak up everything you can to help you become as successful as possible.

Assignments and Expectations

As you progress through the book, prepare yourself mentally to carefully review the concepts and practice what you learn. Above all, proceed with the intent to succeed! If you do this, you'll be very happy with the results.

The material in this book is available in both written and audio formats. It is designed to maximize learning for adults and three important ways:

1. Convenience
We know you are busy at work and home. The audio versions of these chapters allow you to listen as you go through your day–as you commute to work, run on the treadmill, prepare dinner, or relax at home. Listen while you work out, do laundry, or mow the lawn. When you listen while accomplishing other activities, you benefit from the material without having to set aside long hours for dedicated reading. Using this convenient learning method, you are more likely to read and focus on what you're learning.

2. Spaced Repetition
People learn through repetition. Songs that get stuck in your head are there because you've heard or sung them over and over.

You can tap the same learning power by listening to each chapter a minimum of six times. At least one of those times, read the written material as you listen. Take notes and highlight sections that stand out to you, including ideas you agree with or disagree with. Write down questions that come to mind or action items you'd like to try.

3. Multisensory Perception

Learning is most effective when it involves multiple senses. This book engages your senses of sight and hearing through written and recorded materials. Taking notes and keeping a journal involves touch (kinesthetic learning).

Short-term goals, activities, and practice are designed to provide the practical experience that makes the effect of this program permanent. This book helps you develop new skills that can increase your value as an employee in a professional setting. However, it is also filled with information you can apply in all areas of your life: parenting, volunteer work, relationships – just about anywhere. You'll find yourself thinking about the chapters as you go through your day. During the week, you will find many opportunities to put these ideas into action. Consciously practice your new skills at those times, and you will further develop your leadership skills for work.

There is no magic formula for leadership. No one can go to work for you, or be a good team member for you. Likewise, no one can do the work in this book for you. Put your heart into what you learn, and you will realize every possible benefit of your investment. We promise to make your experience organized and meaningful, with interesting tools and activities to help you become an excellent leader.

Conscious growth and development always begin with assessment. Where are you now as a leader, and where do you want to go? This book may cause you to take a look inward, which will help you to stretch and grow. Be prepared for your assessment of yourself to feel a little messy and uncomfortable. Self-discovery can seem awkward, but it's very important if you want to achieve success in any area of your life.

The workplace is rich with opportunity, and you can take advantage of it. All you have to do is make a decision to reach out and grasp it. You have the power to shape your work into meaningful successes, both for you and your organization. Imagine what it will feel like to go to work each day with new skills that help you accomplish things you might have only thought about up to now. You could be the one who helps bring others together to achieve important tasks. Your influence as a leader will be a positive element in your relationships, your projects, and your organization's advancement. As you grow in these leadership skills, you will have much to offer the world. Lead on!

Chapter 1
Basic Communication

What Does it Mean to be a Leader?

What is your title? Does it include the word "leader?" Probably not. We don't usually call leaders by name. But in some way, you are probably a leader. No matter what your position, whether you are an intern, a customer service representative, a project manager, or an administrative assistant, you can be a leader. Personal leadership is the ability to provide guidance and assistance to others, and everyone does that at some level.

The power of personal leadership is called on by people in all walks of life. We see leaders in many different environments: homes, communities, schools, clubs, families, groups of friends, and places of business. You activate the power of leadership when you help someone understand how to do a job better. You're serving as a leader when you take responsibility for the performance of your department or team, even when the work is being criticized. You harness the power of leadership when you mentor a new member of your team or help anyone learn something new.

Good leaders tend to have doubts, but they commit to the path they believe is right, even when it's not easy. You're a leader when you stick with a task, no matter how difficult it is. You are being a leader when you communicate your vision to others, inspire them to embrace it as their own, and motivate them to work with you to achieve that vision.

What does a leader look like? Think about successful community leaders or effective business leaders you've observed or read about. What qualifications and characteristics do they have?

You might have noticed leaders often have very diverse qualities. Even among highly successful people, leaders can demonstrate seemingly opposite leadership styles. Maybe one effective leader you know is obsessed with detail and control, while another focuses on building trust and confidence through collaboration with others.

Leaders begin with a clear understanding of what they want to achieve; then they make a plan and influence others to get on board. Leaders make things happen! No matter what position you hold in your organization, as you carry out your daily tasks (planning, organizing, creating, communicating, directing, monitoring), your team and your superiors will count on you to use influence effectively – to provide leadership.

Communications Skills are a Foundation

Think of someone you know who is a great communicator. The ability to communicate often goes along with other positive qualities. This person probably has a positive attitude in all circumstances. There's a good chance he or she always looks for ways to make things better. These qualities no doubt have an impact on both professional and personal life for the person you're thinking of. Does this person perform well at work? Does he or she have good relationships and other outcomes in life? The answer is probably yes.

Why is communication so important? The answer is that it leads to mutual understanding...which leads to stronger relationships...which leads to better organizations, enhanced friendships, and more cohesive families. The good news is that these skills can be learned with the right kind of practice.

Effective communication is more than knowing the right things to say. The most important skills for communicating well are actually asking the right questions and truly listening. You don't have to become an impressive public speaker to communicate well. These are skills you can use every day in every conversation you have.

As a leader, communicating and collaborating with intent is the way you use your influence to bring people together and make things happen.

More Than Words Can Say

Leaders use many different tools to influence and inspire others – and get things done. Communication is one of the most important leadership tools. Success as a communicator is often directly related to success as a leader.

Dr. Albert Mehrabian is a prominent professor emeritus of psychology at the University of California in Los Angeles. He published a study proving people make judgments about others based on three aspects of communication:

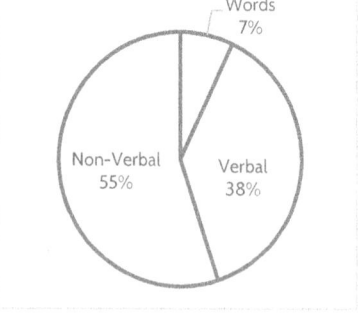

- Words
- Tone of voice
- Nonverbal behavior

Dr. Mehrabian's study showed words account for just 7% of what a listener understands about a person who is speaking. The remaining 93% of a listener's understanding is influenced by the speaker's body language and tone of voice.

Let's take a closer look at this to help you begin thinking about ways you can use communication to connect better with people around you…and become a better leader.

What Influences Meaning?

Leadership means successfully expressing ideas that influence others. How could you use Dr. Mehrabian's findings to make sure what you say is what other people hear?

According to Dr. Mehrabian, certain communication factors dictate how successfully meaning is communicated from one person to another. In this chapter, we'll discuss the factors that have the greatest impact on being an effective leader.

Leaders who successfully influence others learn how to consciously use each of these aspects of communication to move individuals–and the group–in the direction they need to go.

Choose Words Carefully

"The sales department is waiting for your report."

Important information is missing here! Who in the sales department is waiting for the report? When do they need it? Which report is needed? Successfully communicating in a professional setting means carefully choosing the words you use in emails, daily conversations, and meetings. It means saying enough, but not too much. Use complete thoughts and accurate words to clarify your message and avoid misunderstandings.

Imagine you are the person who is listening to you. How can you use words in the content of your message to help the person understand exactly what you need? Once you have chosen the right words, speak clearly, directly, and simply.

"Please deliver the January purchasing report to Jeremy in sales by 4 o'clock today, so we will have it for our staff meeting."

The words you choose reflect more than facts. Words also convey feelings. They can show respect, excitement, disappointment, agreement, and many other emotions, which adds to the power of your message. Words also can convey destructive feelings that undermine your message: anger, frustration, ridicule, or disrespect.

What kinds of words would you choose to refer to female office managers and receptionists in your company? Referring to them as "girls" is disrespectful. Referring to them as "colleagues" or "coworkers" shows respect.

The Power of Your Voice
The words you use are important, but the way you say them has an even greater impact on how well a listener understands your message. Dr. Mehrabian's study revealed that 38% of meaning comes from the way words are spoken – in other words, tone of voice. Qualities of speech such as volume, speed, and pitch communicate deeper meaning behind your words.

When you were a child, what tone of voice did your parents use to let you know they were unhappy with you? You probably didn't have to hear the words to know you were in trouble.

Tone and inflection make your voice a powerful communication tool. You can use it to convey feelings such as confidence and sincerity, which help build trust among your colleagues. Does the tone of your voice come across as upbeat, affirming, and positive, or does it suggest you are uncertain, angry, and frustrated?

Your intent can be misinterpreted easily if your tone of voice contradicts the content of your message. If a store clerk says, "Have a nice day," in a monotone voice, you probably will interpret it to mean, "This is what I've been trained to say to you at the end of the transaction, and I could care less about your day."

Can You Hear Me Now?
When you communicate by phone, your listener can't see important visual clues. Your word choices and tone of voice become especially important. They are the only clues a listener can use to understand your message properly.

Before you place a call, prepare for the conversation by writing down all the topics you plan to cover. This will give you confidence during the call and avoid awkward pauses caused by trying to remember what you want to say. If you need to address a long list of topics, or if you want the full attention of the person you're calling, schedule a phone appointment. This gives the other person time to prepare and an opportunity to choose a place to talk without distractions. With this preparation, your call will be more productive.

Good phone communication begins with a professional greeting, so your listener knows you are calling about business. Speak clearly, at a rate and volume that help your words come through clearly. Ask if it's a good time to talk. If it's not, ask if you can return the call later, then be sure to follow through. It's much better to defer a phone conversation to another time than to risk miscommunication because either of you feels distracted or rushed.

Approach business conversations on your cell phone with the same consideration you use in all of your professional communications. Sometimes it's better not to answer your phone at all, such as when you really don't have time to talk. Consider not answering if you are someplace with too much going on to have a thoughtful conversation.

Never answer your cell phone:
- in a meeting
- in a restroom
- in busy traffic
- when you are talking with someone in person
- in a loud environment where you can't hear the caller

Just as you would in a face-to-face conversation, it's important to keep negative emotions in check during phone calls. Even if you are tired or frustrated, you can't allow destructive emotions to come through as you communicate with others. This means you must be aware of the power of your voice and the words you choose. Use them effectively to set a positive tone for communication.

Did You See What She Said?
You've probably heard the expression, "If looks could kill." You may even have received one of those "killer" looks!

Nonverbal or visual communication, such as the "killer" look, have a huge impact on your message – more than any other aspect of communication, including the words you choose and the way you say them. Studies show 55% of meaning is derived from the visual messages your listener sees in facial expressions and body language.

When you speak with someone face-to-face, you might not realize the impact and power of your nonverbal, visual language. Do you sometimes wave your hands to emphasize a point? We have all opened our eyes wide in astonishment, shaken our heads in sympathy, and crossed our arms when we disagreed. It is vital to become aware of your own nonverbal messages as you communicate. You also can learn to read the facial expressions and body language of others to better understand what they are trying to say.

Everyone has a unique way of communicating nonverbally. The same nonverbal signal might mean something different to two different people. Let's say you notice Nate fidgeting and looking around the room during a conversation. You ask him what he is thinking, and you learn he doesn't agree with you. Now that you know this, you can give Nate the opportunity to express his opinion.

In another situation, you may notice Susan displaying the same behavior. When you talk with her, you learn she is distracted because she is feeling overworked. This gives you the opportunity to help her resolve her problem and focus better on the next conversation.

As a leader, it's your job to look for nonverbal clues and use them to understand your listeners and improve your communication with one another. You might learn Amanda turns sullen and quiet when faced with change. To the perceptive coworker, this is a signal to provide her with more information or encourage her to ask questions. Is Jake concentrating when he closes his eyes, or is he simply tired? When Noah slumps down in his chair and crosses his arms, is it because he's angry or is he feeling a lack of confidence?

As a leader, you must develop both the ability to read body language in others and be aware of signals you send with your own body language. Successful salespeople are very good at this. They know how to read visual cues from potential customers. And they know how to use their own body language to deliver messages more effectively and inspire customers to buy.

Technology's Impact on Communication

Tell us in your own sissy words how your feelings were hurt.

This surprising line was included in a humorous student report form sent to elementary school parents. The form, which included many other sarcastic prompts, was mistakenly attached to a parent message. We don't know for sure what happened, but we can imagine.

The parents might have guessed it was a mistake, but they would, no doubt, feel offended anyway. Remember, they have no way of seeing the secretary's embarrassment in her facial expressions, tone of voice, or body language. They were forced to fill in the blanks for themselves, probably wondering why she would have sent such a thing. They might even have wondered if the secretary thought parents would share her frustration that students often make a big deal of hurt feelings.

No matter what led to this mistake, it's fair to say the secretary had been careless. The parents were, at a minimum, confused and, at a maximum, hurt and angry. Email is a convenient way to communicate. However, in this case, using email led to disaster. This story underscores the care with which we need to choose and use methods of communication in the business world.

Email is an important tool that allows colleagues to communicate with one another efficiently. Text messages are another important primary business communication method. However, it's essential to know why you are using a particular method – and to use it very carefully, so it supports your objectives the way you expect it to.

Before sending an email or text, ask yourself whether you are choosing the most effective means of communication. Are you simply avoiding personal interaction? Is there potential for someone to misunderstand what you're saying? Are you trying to convey too much using a method of communication designed for simple messaging? Have you double checked your words and attachments to make sure they correctly reflect your message?

Email and texts are best used to communicate factual messages with brief information, such as meeting and deadline reminders and details you want everyone to have in writing. For lengthier or more substantial discussions, face-to-face meetings or phone calls are better options.

Email Best Practices

To use email effectively, first think about the reasons you are writing, and then carefully construct your message.

Treat email as you would other kinds of written business communication.
Your message carries more weight when you use proper grammar, spelling, capitalization, and punctuation. Reserve smiley faces and spelling shortcuts for personal messages.

Write a specific subject line.
A good subject line describes the content of your email accurately and clearly, with key terms that make it easier to search for the message in the future.

Be clear and concise.
Communication experts say people are most likely to read and understand emails of 10 lines or less, with a limited number of topics. Readers tend to skim over longer emails, which could cause them to miss some of the content.

Use an easy-to-understand format.
Consider organizing your material with bullet points, lists, and short paragraphs. Focus only on one or two ideas in each email.

Stick to the facts.
Email communication relies solely on words. Written messages can be easily misinterpreted if the content is emotionally charged or based on opinion.

Limit attachments.
Just as limited topics help readers understand your message, a limited number of attachments avoids confusion. It also avoids overloading your recipient's email system. Don't forget to make sure you're using the correct attachment!

Double-check addresses.
We've all heard horror stories about someone accidentally sending emails to the wrong person or to everyone in the company. Or accidentally sending a private message to everyone. Depending on the content, a blunder like this could be a career-ender. Carefully check the address of each recipient before pressing Send.

Proofread, proofread, proofread.
Does your message make sense? If you are requesting action from the recipient, are your expectations clear? Check for proper

word use, grammar, and punctuation. Don't rely solely on spell check. The following sentence passes spell check, but the underlined words are incorrect:

> "...<u>butt</u> the <u>principal</u> reason we purchase paper from Company X <u>verses</u> Company Y is <u>there</u> promise of on-time delivery."

Text with the Best

Whether your message is personal or professional, when you need to communicate facts quickly, texting is often the most effective method. Limit texts to timely facts people need to know fast, such as the time and place of a meeting or the fact that you've been delayed.

Texting can be used creatively in business to improve efficiency. Conference staff can use texting to notify each another of their current locations on a resort property. A deskbound receptionist can text clerical staff to request supplies. Texting can help you respond faster, and it's easy for the receiver of your message to reply quickly by texting back. A 2012 study found that texting was the highest rated contact method for customer satisfaction out of all other customer communication channels.

In some situations, texting is not appropriate. It's rude to carry on a private text conversation during a meeting or event. It's tempting, but disrespectful, to send text messages to avoid an emotional in-person conversation.

Some people have a bad habit of not answering texts. Remember, good communication involves both giving and receiving information. The process isn't complete until you let the other person know their text has been received.

Can you imagine doing without email and texting? Both can be amazing communication tools for business when used correctly, in the proper context. They are so easy to use–and convenient! Make sure the convenience and speed of email and texting doesn't lead to mistakes. Also, avoid the temptation to make them your only forms of communication or to substitute technology for face-to-face interactions.

Just Add Video

Sometimes it's not possible to meet face-to-face. Clients and colleagues working in offices far removed from one another miss out on important visual clues that aid communication. Luckily, video conferencing allows us to conduct screen-to-screen conversations with both individuals and groups. Mobile apps are best suited for one-on-one conversations. Sophisticated videoconferencing systems are used to communicate with groups in conference rooms or auditoriums with large screens.

These technologies don't take the place of in-person communication. But they do add visual clues that help us translate the messages coming our way.

When you meet with someone electronically, conduct yourself as if you were meeting in person in a local conference room. The same principles of effective business communication apply:

1. Be punctual and professional.
2. Be aware of your personal appearance and the appearance of your surroundings.
3. Make sure nothing in the room is distracting.
4. Make sure you can hear and be heard.
5. Focus on each person speaking, and use good conversation etiquette.
6. Write an agenda and stick to it.

7. Summarize assignments and action steps.
8. Let others know you need privacy and should not be interrupted.

Now you understand how words, verbal messages, and nonverbal messages impact communication. These aspects of language are just one part of becoming a better communicator.

Communication's Forgotten Side: Listening

When you think about communicating with someone, you probably first think about the things we've been discussing in this lesson–ways to push your message out there and get your ideas across so you can get things done.

We tend to forget about another very important part of communication. It's often one of the least developed professional skills: effective listening. It's the silent side of communication, but doing it well can make all the difference in the world. Ironically, becoming proficient in using this passive skill requires intense practice and dedication.

The most successful leaders develop a keen sense of listening to not only what a person says, but to the meaning behind their words. This is known as active listening. It requires the full attention and involvement of the listener.

Passive listening is the opposite of active listening. Passive listeners are uninterested, preoccupied, busy, bored, pressured, or otherwise distracted. This type of listening can result in distorted messages and misunderstandings. Passive listening can even lead to a lack of respect and damaged relationships.

Sometimes what people don't say is even more important than what they do say. As a conversation is taking place, an active listener goes beyond language and considers much more:

- Personality and mood of the speaker

- Time of day
- Circumstances surrounding the message
- The person's work and home stressors
- Background noise
- Body language
- Many other factors

Even in the best of situations, becoming aware of these bits of information and applying them to the speaker's words can be a challenge. The more you practice this skill, the better you'll get at using it to improve your communication abilities.

The Writing-Speaking-Listening Journey Toward Influence

Have you ever wondered how great leaders accomplish great things? Here's the secret: They influence people and inspire change by communicating effectively and taking action.

The importance of communication can't be overstated, which is why it's the topic of this first lesson. Masterful communication allows a leader to effectively connect with her colleagues and coworkers, with customers and vendors, and with her superiors. Communication is crucial to her success and to her company's success. Unfortunately, research shows most of us are just not good at communicating, in spite of communication-enhancing technology; in spite of all the methods and styles of communicating available to us. But don't let that stop you!

Most great leaders did not naturally become successful communicators. They had to work at it. As a professional, if you want to, you can work at it, too; and learn how to use communication to reach your goals, your team's goals, and your company's goals. It begins with nurturing a desire to improve. What motivates you to improve? Think about the people you work with. Imagine how great it would feel to be the one who leads them to success in all kinds of ways. That's a perfect motivation.

Great leaders invest time and effort to build relationships based on trust, honesty, and compassion; and communication helps with that. Use communication to show respect and a true desire to understand each person. An effective leader or team member genuinely likes people, actively listens, values the ideas and opinions of others, and actively seeks opportunities to communicate.

Communication is just the beginning, though. The journey toward effective leadership will challenge and stretch you in many ways. Allow yourself to feel motivated to influence! Imagine yourself growing into a leadership role that fits you just right and accomplishing great things with others. You might even find you aspire to greater roles in the future.

Are you consciously and intentionally working to become a better communicator? Are you ready to activate the power of leadership and make a positive difference for your coworkers, your customers, and your company?

Three Things to Remember

1. Regardless of your job title, you have the ability to lead through the effective use of all methods of communication and creating mutual understanding.

2. Leaders who successfully influence others learn how to consciously use each aspect of communication to move individuals - and the group - in the direction they need to go.

3. Email and texts are best used to communicate factual messages with brief information. For lengthier or more substantial discussions, face-to-face meetings or phone calls are better options.

Putting it to Work

- Write down three valuable ideas from the chapter.

- What one thing can you do to start implementing each idea?

- What impact will taking action have on you or the team you lead?

Chapter 2
The Cost of Keeping Score

Why Businesses Need Good Communicators

Think about the way we do business today. Communication with coworkers and customers happens by email, text, and social media. Collaboration often is defined as two or more people working on the same file stored in the cloud. Face time isn't a look-you-in-the-eye meeting; it's an app. When we want to get really personal, we leave a voicemail.

In striving for efficiency, we've created a work environment that can seem cold and impersonal. Yet, a funny thing has happened on the way to our tech-heavy, app-happy, screen-interfacing business model; we have begun to value even more those team members who take a personal approach to working with others. Whether we work from home, or a cubicle, the cab of a truck, or on a production line, we want others to know more about us than our employee ID. Even with technology at our disposal, relationships and collaboration are more important than ever.

People who experience the greatest success know their success is determined by their ability to be an effective team member – to collaborate and communicate with others in the right way to get work done. In most organizations, communication takes place among members of teams. Some teams are small, such as project teams. An entire company can be considered a team. Businesses rely on the efforts of many different people, positions, and departments coming together to fully realize the organization's goals. Those goals can't be reached if every person in the organization is working completely independent of others. Businesses value employees who demonstrate the ability to work as an effective team member.

When we have opportunities to collaborate and work with a team, interpersonal problems are bound to surface. We all have different styles of communication and different approaches to doing work. People don't always see eye-to-eye. Difficulties with communication can be stressful and also keep the team from reaching its goals.

Placing Blame and Keeping Score

How do you feel when a coworker is being difficult? You might tell yourself, "If only she would stop being so difficult, we could actually work together!" If you live with a spouse or roommate, do you ever find yourself fighting and think, "If only he would listen better, we wouldn't fight as often."

It's human nature to find ourselves free of blame, with positive intentions, while counting the many faults and missteps of the other party. This helps us feel justified in the negative feelings we have about the other person. We sometimes keep a long list of wrongs someone has committed in the back of our mind, just in case we need to come up with a reason to be angry with that person in the future.

In the field of psychology, the human phenomenon that causes us to blame others is explained by the Fundamental

Attribution Theory. The theory comes into play when we automatically attribute the root cause of a problem to another person's negative or selfish behaviors, and feel justified in assigning blame. If we choose to never forget these perceived selfish behaviors, it's called "keeping score."

Scorekeeping sets off an endless cycle of mistrust and unprincipled behaviors. It starts with one perceived wrongdoing, which causes you to behave badly, and that in turn causes the other person to mistrust you and act badly toward you.

Each new act causes more perceived slights, which causes more mistrust and bad behavior. Eventually neither party is acting ethically, and each person is conveniently reinforcing what the other thinks about them. Consider the following scenario:

Marge and Shana
Marge is annoyed that Shana, her coworker in the next cubicle, plays music while she works. Marge believes it must be impossible for Shana to get any work done, because she herself can't think straight while the music is playing…and there is a wall between them! Marge begins by sending subtle hints. Maybe she can get Shana to realize the music is making it hard to focus on her work, without really having to say anything. Marge says to Shana, "Wow, you sure listen to a lot of music, Shana!" Shana responds, saying it helps her concentrate and drowns out the office noise. She keeps playing her music.

As Marge's frustration mounts, she's asked to work collaboratively with Shana on an upcoming project. Marge discovers important data relating to Shana's part of the project, but she is frustrated with Shana and doesn't feel like sharing. So, she conveniently "forgets" to share it. She justifies this to herself by choosing to believe Shana's music is the problem.

> *If Shana would work a little harder instead of listening to music all day, she would find the data herself. It's not as though she doesn't have access to the data.*

When the project is turned in to their manager, the manager is upset with Shana for not including the data, and Shana suddenly realizes Marge kept the information from her. This confirms the impression that Shana has always had of Marge: she is self-serving and not a team player – Marge is out to get her. Shana now makes a point to play her music even louder, because she has heard from others in the office that it annoys Marge. Shanna feels completely justified in her behavior because of Marge's behavior during the project. They continue to find ways to provoke negative behaviors in each other, which in turn confirms their negative views about each other.

In this situation, neither individual originally acted with negative intent. They were each just trying to meet their own needs and work in an environment conducive to their work style. Yet, as the situation escalated, they each began to keep score, tallying up the other's perceived wrongdoings and then attempting to even the score. It's likely both Shana and Marge were able to convince other coworkers of their position and gain support as a victim of wrongdoing. And so it begins to affect the entire department.

The Blame Stain

The expanding negative effects that result from blaming someone else for the problems you are experiencing. It takes more work to clean up a blame stain than it does to stop the blaming and seek understanding.

What's the Payoff?

Why do we feel the need to keep score? Why would Shana and Marge engage in such inefficient behaviors – actions that undermine the organization's goals and relationships with coworkers? It can't be that they enjoy conflict and a tense working environment. Can it? Is there something each of them enjoyed about the conflict? Is it possible they each gained something personally through their negative interactions?

Unfortunately as human beings, we do enjoy a certain amount of conflict and problems in our lives. It gives us stories to share. It can add a little excitement to a boring day. It gives us something to complain about. This need sometimes overshadows the destruction blame can cause.

Scorekeeping can begin innocently when we perceive a meaningless situation to have more meaning than it actually was intended to have. In other words, scorekeeping often begins when we blow things out of proportion. Consider Marge and Shana again. Shana's playing of the music was not intended to anger her coworkers. She simply was trying to drown out office noise so she could work. Yet, if others interpret Shana's behavior as an attempt to annoy them, they could begin to make unflattering assumptions about Shana's personality, work ethic, and desire (or lack of desire) to be courteous.

Remember the Fundamental Attribution Theory. It's human nature to automatically assign blame to someone else when we're faced with a problem or difficult situation. We do it as a means to protect ourselves. If we can justify blaming another person, we do not have to admit our own wrongdoings and mistakes.

In a similar way, if we haven't done something we should have done, or if we *have* done something we *shouldn't have*, we might unconsciously feel the need to justify our own questionable behavior. We need a reason to feel okay about what we've done or haven't done. In the end, if we can find someone else to blame, we don't have to take responsibility ourselves. And, if it's someone else's problem, we don't have to find a way out of the cycle of unprincipled behaviors.

Next time you are involved in a drama you might have helped create, try to understand what is causing your own actions. Ask yourself if your behavior is a part of the problem. Consider whether you have gained any personal satisfaction from perpetuating the cycle. Most people would say they hate the drama or they are exhausted by it. Yet, they continue to engage in behaviors that feed the fire.

Trying a Different Approach
It's not important to end the cycle of scorekeeping if you don't care about fixing the relationship or have nothing to gain by working with the other person. However, because organizations get things done when people work together on a set of common goals, you may need to find a way to avoid this problem.

In a perfect organization, what is good for one department or person is also good for the group. Department level benefits have an impact on the overall goals and vision of the organization. Some organizations are very good at nurturing a sense of shared successes. If we take into consideration the needs of 1) the organization, 2) the people, and 3) the customers, the outcome is a win/win for all involved. This is an impossible task if individuals are keeping score and are more concerned about their own personal agendas than collaborating.

To achieve a different outcome, you must be willing to take a different approach. You have to nurture a desire to help create a positive work environment and/or personal environment – even when someone disappoints you, has a different opinion than you, or angers you. Having a positive impact on the interpersonal environment of your company means taking personal responsibility for your own actions and opening yourself to the other person's point of view. This is our "moment of truth." Some might call it an "Oh crap!" moment. We have two choices: We can try to protect ourselves by blaming others or we can seek understanding of the situation.

When our immediate response is to blame others:
We instantly excuse our role in the problem. As a result, we don't take time to ask questions and listen so we can discover what caused the problem. Instead, we are focused on placing blame, rather than finding a solution.

When we consciously seek to understand the situation:
We're not interested in assigning blame. We talk to the other individual and hear his thoughts and perspective on the situation. Without the conflict creating a barrier between us, we can work together to find real solutions to more important problems.

    Look back on a recent situation in your life that was a moment of truth. Think of a time when things did not go as expected or someone failed to keep their end of the bargain. What did you choose to do at that moment? Did you do nothing? Did you immediately decide the other person was to blame? Or did you take time to ask questions and listen to the other person's side of the story? You might discover there is more to the situation than you originally thought.
    When you take a different approach, seeking to understand, you might find out what really happened without creating a "blame stain" you later have to clean up.

The following flowchart illustrates the outcomes of different responses to a moment of truth. Choosing to do nothing is a dead end. If you respond by placing the blame solely on the other person, you've missed an opportunity to build trusting relationships and you have undermined your ability to work collaboratively with others.

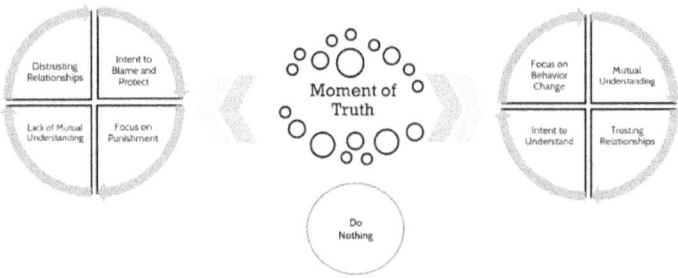

If your intent is not to find someone to blame, but to listen and understand the situation, you will pick up the phone to have a conversation with someone or walk to their desk to discuss the situation face-to-face. You become focused on determining what thoughts or behaviors need to change – yours and/or theirs – so everyone's expectations can be met in the future. At the moment of truth, you can respond in a way that builds trust with others and makes them more open to sharing a solution rather than focusing on the problem.

You never know when a moment of truth will arise. Remember: you get to decide how you respond, and your response can make all the difference.

The Conversation: A Formula for Mutual Understanding

Let's say you decide to respond to a moment of truth with the intent to understand. What should you do first? No matter what the reason for the conflict, choosing to understand and move forward in a positive way often means having an honest conversation with the other person. It's usually not easy. Confronting someone who has disappointed you or frustrated you can be stressful. You don't know how the other person will respond. Will he or she get angry or defensive? Will it make the situation worse? What if you are caught off-guard and suddenly feel unprepared and vulnerable? Your own less-than-honorable motivations could be exposed, and you might feel embarrassed.

Many have found a formula called "The Conversation" to be useful during difficult interactions. The formula encourages dialogue and mutual understanding. It allows the other person to share his or her side of the story. It gives you an opportunity to gather information without making assumptions. It also invites the other person to participate in determining an appropriate resolution and working together on a plan to move forward. The Conversation enhances understanding and creates buy-in.

The Conversation
1. Say what you were expecting.
2. Say what you noticed.
3. Say "Help me understand."
4. Agree on a plan to meet a mutual expectation.
5. Explain why it is important.

Let's take a look at how The Conversation works in practice.
You rely on Ethan to email you his team's production numbers by Friday at 8 a.m. For the past two weeks, you haven't received Ethan's numbers until Friday afternoon, but you need the numbers earlier so you can prepare a weekly report and deliver it to your manager.

- **You**: "Hey, Ethan, you know the production numbers are due by Friday at 8 a.m. (Step 1), but for the past two weeks I haven't received them until the afternoon. (Step 2) Will you help me understand what happened?" (Step 3)

- **Ethan**: "I know! My Fridays have been crazy for the past two weeks because several people on my team are on vacation. Then I forgot about the production numbers until it was after the time they were due."

- **You**: "I understand. Is there anything you could do in the future to make sure I have your numbers by 8 a.m.? (Step 4)"

- **Ethan**: "I put a reminder on my calendar for Thursday afternoon, so I'm not waiting until Friday morning to collect the data."

- **You**: "Thank you Ethan! I really appreciate that. I've got to have the numbers by 8 a.m. so I can prepare the weekly report for my manager. (Step 5)"

In this example, you led the conversation with the intent to understand the situation. You did not immediately jump to the conclusion that Ethan did not care about getting the production numbers to you on time. You weren't looking for someone to blame. You were seeking a solution.

Believe in Positive Intent

Once you begin to practice and use The Conversation, one very important condition is fundamental to using it successfully.

Before you even begin to ask the right questions and create mutual understanding, you first have to find a way within yourself to believe the other person has positive intentions. You must embrace this attitude - no matter how difficult it might be.

When you've made a mistake, forgotten to do something, or offended another person, what was your intention? Did you purposely make that mistake? Let's say you forgot to make a phone call to the customer service department. Did you forget on purpose to frustrate someone? When you made that comment the other day about someone's work, did you mean to offend them? Most likely, that was not your intention.

When we interpret someone else's behaviors, why do we often assume they were intentionally trying to make us feel bad or make our jobs more difficult? Remember the Fundamental Attribution Theory. We have a predisposition for attributing a negative experience to someone else's faults or shortcomings. We look for someone else to blame.

War is famous for misunderstood intentions and quickness to blame. During World War II, Japan's ruler was asked by reporters if he would surrender. He used the word "mokusatsu" in his response, which meant "We withhold comment." The answer was mistranslated to mean "Not worthy of comment" and published throughout the world. Some people questioned whether the message was correct, but most instantly assumed Japan's intent was negative. U.S. officials were pressured to respond strongly and deployment of the atomic bomb was authorized.

How might history have changed if someone had considered Japan's ruler's message from an attitude of belief that others have positive intent? Even enemies reach a point of willingness to comply. Japan was being encouraged to surrender by many of the leaders of the world. If someone had thought to question the answer, it might have saved many lives.

The good news is that, in your life, you can eliminate the damage caused by blaming others when you instead choose to assume others have good intentions – just like you. To believe others have the same basic wants, needs, and fears you have. To believe your coworkers' needs, wants, and fears are just as important as yours. First, you must make a conscious choice to have a positive attitude and open yourself to seeing things from a different perspective.

We can provide you with the right questions to ask and a format to ask those questions, but if you have already made up your mind about the other person's intentions and believe you know why they acted in the manner they did, you won't truly be open to hearing and understanding their perspective. You will not have the power to turn things around.

Asking the Right Questions

What does it mean to facilitate? By definition, it means to help or make possible. One dictionary adds this: "...to assist the progress of." This is a little different from what we first think of when we think of facilitating. We tend to believe facilitation simply means completing a task or assignment. As you can see from these definitions, it's more than that. It's about process, support, and opportunity. In this case, facilitation is a tool you or anybody can use to assist in progress and create mutual understanding.

Facilitation is closely tied to communication. If you learn and apply certain facilitating techniques, you will improve your communication skills. One technique is to ask questions or use open statements strategically to lead people toward a desired understanding or goal.

Questions are designed to raise awareness, challenge thinking, provide options, or supply information about a situation. Ultimately, questions can bring about a new understanding or viewpoint. Questions are the language of facilitation. There is an art to asking questions and listening like you mean it. If you learn how to ask facilitating questions, it will become a skill you can use to help you work toward any goal with any person in any situation.

Questions use a specific kind of expressive, probing language that nurtures a shared understanding and responsibility. The process of facilitation begins with asking a good question. The next step is listening with an intent to understand while the other person is responding. Finally, a facilitator asks good follow-up questions. These steps create a continuous discovery - conversation loop. The deeper the question, the deeper the listening; the deeper the listening, the deeper the next question. As we dig into issues together using this facilitative process, we make new discoveries together. The learning is never one-sided. It is a co-creation process that produces empathy, trust, and collaboration.

The Power of Authentic Questions

Successful facilitation requires us to empower others and build consensus. One of the best ways to do this is to ask questions. Not just any questions, but really good questions that stimulate insight and understanding.

Research has shown the most successful people make this kind of question-asking an integral part of their lives. In essence, they allow themselves to be respectfully curious. Practicing respectful curiosity and using questions to learn more from and about the people around you can help you build relationships. It can help you bring people together to work toward goals successfully.

Imagine yourself asking more questions to:
- Look at situations from a different point of view.
- Sort out where others are coming from.
- Probe deeper into the motivations, perspectives, and experiences of others.
- Bring an "unspeakable" question to the surface to resolve it.
- Challenge the status quo and move the conversation to the next level.

Nothing kills a conversation faster than a throwaway question that doesn't invite thoughtful response or further dialogue. Journalists learn early that an interview goes nowhere when they ask questions interviewees can answer with "yes" or "no." Consider rephrasing these types of questions. For example, rather than asking, "Are you frustrated?" ask "Why is this situation so frustrating for you?"

Sometimes a yes/no question is necessary for clarification, but the best questions engage and intrigue the person being asked. A conversation should have movement, with ideas flowing naturally. Good questions make that happen and propel the conversation forward. Use the following types of questions and statements to encourage participation.

Closed questions:
Can be answered with one or two words, and can be useful as follow-up questions to gain clarification. Closed questions also can be useful to help introverted or reserved people begin to engage in the process.

- "So you don't feel this is a workable solution?"
- "Did you say you would be willing to work with Jackie on that part of the project?"

Open questions:
Invite more than a one-word response. Many times they start with who, what, when, where, why, or how.
- "How would this scenario impact your department's productivity?"
- "What would happen if you moved the copier from accounting to marketing?"

Encouraging statements:
Welcome elaboration. They send the person a cue that you want to know more.
- "Explain how you can get accounting to agree to move the copier."
- "Give me an example of how we might streamline the process, as you suggested."
- "Help me understand how to communicate this information in a better way."

Listening Like You Mean It

Even the best questions seem inauthentic if posed by someone who is harried and doesn't seem interested in the response. To facilitate a conversation successfully, we need to be sure we are encouraging, and even expecting, the other person to engage with us. One way to indicate our interest and expectation is through active listening.

When you're in a facilitating conversation, focus *only* on the conversation. Remember, you need to listen like you mean it. Close the folder in front of you and turn away from your computer screen. Turn off your phone. If possible, hold the conversation in a quiet, non-distracting environment where you won't be interrupted. Look directly at the other person and indicate your interest in what they're saying by leaning in and nodding occasionally. Make sure your posture is open (unfold your arms and face the person directly).

Listen to every word the person says and pay attention to nonverbal communication. Don't cut him off or spend time formulating your own response, when you should be listening. In fact, you can demonstrate your thoughtful engagement by pausing after he finishes speaking and saying, "You have given me some things to think about. Give me a minute to consider what you said."

Guidelines for responding to questions:
- Be positive, not angry.
- Ask for specific questions or examples.
- Redirect questions.
- Encourage the person to participate.
- Ask for a new point of view.
- Paraphrase for understanding.
- Never say the person is wrong.

If you are facilitating a conversation with a more introverted person who likes to take her time to think and consider before responding, you might want to ask your questions, and then meet later to discuss her answers.

Putting it All Together

So far, the focus of this lesson has been "leading with the intent to understand." However, for someone initiating a conversation, the intent is almost always "to be understood." During the facilitation process, even though your initial intent is to understand, when you ask the right questions, you will likely have an opportunity to be understood as well.

In the following scenario, Sophie is kicked out of the company's software program as she tries to save a proposal for a client that is due by the end of the day. She heads to speak with her co-worker Jake in IT.

Let's see how this might play out between Sophie and Jake if they use the facilitation process.

- **Sophie:** "Hi Jake, what's the best way to request assistance from your department for the software problems I had today?"

- **Jake:** "I'm sorry you're having trouble with the software. You need to complete a work order to request assistance."

- **Sophie:** "Great. I'll fill out a work order right away. Do you know if others have had similar problems with the software? Any suggestions I could try in the meantime?"

- **Jake:** "Help me understand a little more about the problems you are experiencing."

- **Sophie:** "Twice today, when I tried to save a client folder, it kicked me out of the program. It has become critical at this point, because I have a proposal due to the client by the end of the day."

- **Jake:** "What have you tried so far?"

- **Sophie:** "I restarted my computer once, and then it happened again after that."

- **Jake:** "I have time this afternoon to look at your computer. Would that work for you?"

- **Sophie:** "Yes, I'll be in my office the rest of the day. Thanks for your help."

- **Jake:** "Could you please fill out the work order before I come over to your office? I'm required to have the form for documentation and tracking, so we can better diagnose problems."

- **Sophie:** "Of course. See you this afternoon. Thanks again!"

In our scenario, Sophie continues asking questions, even when she doesn't get the initial response she wanted from Jake. She is willing to follow the work order process, realizing it is a priority to Jake. However, at the same time, she uses questions to create space for mutual understanding. Once Jake understands how critical her need is, he is willing to help.

You Can Stop the Cycle

As you know, one perceived wrongdoing can cause long-lasting rifts between people and departments. If not handled well, this kind of conflict not only jeopardizes the goals of your organization, but it can cause you and others a great deal of pain. It's human nature to blame others for our problems, but blame and miscommunication lead to disaster.

Luckily, you now know about some tools you can use against this destructive force. Can you imagine yourself handling conversations better? Can you see how seeking to understand before doing anything else can collapse barriers between people? If you abandon the need to keep score and learn to manage conversations, it will help you stop the endless cycle of mistrust and unprincipled behaviors.

- First, allow yourself to believe people's intentions are good.
- Then, use different styles of questioning and encouraging statements to seek clarification.
- Then, encourage other people to work with you.
- Finally, identify a mutual understanding of your goals and expectations, and move forward together to achieve your goals.

Three Things to Remember

1. To have the greatest influence as a leader, embrace the belief that others do things with good intentions.

2. Without conflict creating a barrier between us, we can work together to find real solutions to more important problems.

3. If you learn how to ask facilitating questions, it will become a skill you can use to help you work toward any goal with any person in any situation.

Putting it to Work

- Write down three valuable ideas from the chapter.

- What one thing can you do to start implementing each idea?

- What impact will taking action have on you or the team you lead?

Chapter 3
Crucial Conversations

It Begins with a Conversation

Think back to some of the most crucial moments of your life, both good and bad. What do they all have in common? Other than the fact that you were there, it's a good bet nearly every one of those situations involved a conversation – or lack of a conversation.

Those important moments in your life involved people, because in almost every aspect of life, we interact with other people. In our personal lives, we interact with others while we're running our households, raising our children, and spending time with friends and family. Even when we're away from home, we interact with store clerks, service technicians, law enforcement officers, and many others. In most work environments, we have to interact and communicate with people, because we have to rely on others to get our own work done.

Do you work on a team? As we've discussed, to reach team goals, each person in the group must perform part of the work. Collaboration and communication between team members is required. Maybe you work in IT and you have to interact daily to resolve computer issues other people are experiencing. Human resources employees communicate back and forth with nearly every other department in an organization. All of these interactions require communication, and that means conversations.

Communication is easy – until it isn't! Most of us don't take time to think about our approach to communication. We go about our day talking with others and writing messages without being intentional about what we're saying or not saying. Often, we don't realize, until we look back at a situation, where something went wrong. Then, we wonder whether we should have or shouldn't have said one thing or another. Many times, we aren't even aware that our communication style could offend another person.

Imagine the following scenario...
You are working busily in your office, minding your own business. Your coworker interrupts you for the umpteenth time today to tell you more about his kid's athletic abilities. You try to send nonverbal cues to let him know this is starting to get on your nerves and to impress upon him that you are extremely busy. It doesn't stop him from eating up another 15 minutes of your time.

This continues to happen regularly. Eventually, you talk with your boss about the distraction. Your boss talks to your coworker. Now the interactions between you and your coworker are awkward and uncomfortable. You begin to notice other coworkers are avoiding you as well. Has he been talking about you behind your back? What has he said?

Your coworker is confused and frustrated – and a little angry. He was just trying to be friendly and get to know you on a personal level. You both have children, and he thought you might want to talk about this thing you have in common. Doesn't everyone want a little break from their work from time to time?

Why would you go to the boss instead of coming to him? He now thinks you are a jerk for not simply telling him you were busy.

This may seem petty or insignificant. But it's not petty if the situation is negatively affecting you and your coworkers' ability to collaborate. This tense and awkward situation, at least for the moment, might undermine your team's productivity and success. Research shows that 60% to 80% of all difficulties in organizations stem from strained relationships between employees, not from deficits in individual employees' skill or motivation.

Think how powerful it would be for the future of your company if you and your coworkers could learn to interact with people better and make some of those difficulties go away! What if you had responded to your coworker in a different way? Maybe a healthy, yet direct, conversation could have helped you avoid straining this relationship.

Let's consider a different scenario...
You are at home with your spouse watching TV. Your daughter comes into the room and asks to borrow the car again. The last time she did, she left the gas tank empty and was an hour late getting home. You immediately say "No" and refuse to listen to her excuses or pleas. You've had a rough day at work and are not in the mood to argue with her. You tell her no again, and for added emphasis remind her of all the times she has been irresponsible in the past year. She stomps off, hurt and crying, and your spouse is looking at you like you are being unreasonable. You just can't win!

Back at work the next day, you have a one-on-one meeting with your manager. You have been looking forward to this meeting for weeks. You have been wanting to share an idea you believe could improve efficiency in your department and save everyone time and money. You begin to share your idea, and even before you have finished the thought, your manager tells you why it won't work. She moves onto the next topic, dismissing your idea completely.

You feel your face starting to turn red, and your pulse quickens. When you walk out of the meeting, you think of a hundred different things you could have said to keep the conversation going. If you only could've thought of those things at the time, the conversation might have had a different outcome. But it's too late. The opportunity is gone. The emotion of the situation piles on top of the frustration with your daughter, and you're now feeling extremely irritated, discouraged, and maybe a little desperate. To make yourself feel better, you make a mental note to take your time getting your report done next week. If your manager doesn't want to hear your ideas, why would you work hard to meet her deadlines?

The Impact of Conversations

The scenarios we just discussed began with a conversation, or lack thereof, and ended with hurt feelings, criticism, misunderstanding, and frustration. Although conversations give us opportunities to strengthen our relationships, they also have the potential to damage or strain our relationships. When things are going well and there is no pressure, most daily conversations are easy. But what happens when the stakes are high? What do you say when you feel confronted or find yourself in emotionally charged situations? Or when you have a lot to lose or gain?

We all have different styles of communication, and our personal communication style can change in times of conflict or pressure. Some respond by shutting down and not sharing their ideas or opinions. Others take a more direct, sometimes abrasive approach. It becomes more about winning than working to solve the problem at hand.

Unfortunately, not many of us are good at having healthy conversations when we're in the middle of conflict or high-pressure situations. You might be wondering whether it matters how you handle a difficult conversation. Isn't it okay to just do the best you can?

Think about a conversation with a coworker, significant other, child, or friend that didn't go the way you expected. When the conversation was over, you might have thought, "If only I had said this or not said that!" Now you are desperately trying to figure out how to fix the damage you believe you might have just created in that relationship. That's why it matters. The way we handle critical moments in our lives has a direct impact on our relationships with others at home and work. It affects how well our families run and how well our teams function.

Think back to the scenario above with your daughter. The situation continues to escalate. Your spouse hasn't spoken more than a few words to you in the past few weeks, and your daughter snuck out of the house last night. If the previous conversations had been handled differently, would the outcome have been different? With less of an emotional burden, would you then have handled yourself better with your boss?

Now, think back to the scenario between the two coworkers. After the conversation with their manager, whenever the two coworkers have to collaborate on a project, they are hesitant to trust each other. This leads to poor information-sharing and collaboration. They are constantly trying to be the first to figure out how one is trying to mess up the other's part of a project. Their manager is confused as to why the project is behind schedule and missing important information. In meetings, the manager notices people aren't sharing their ideas and opinions as freely as they did before. He begins to realize there is no trust between team members.

Organizations and businesses are made up of people, so it's only natural during the course of our work days that we sometimes face situations requiring difficult conversations. Maybe we disagree with another person's opinion about the way something should be done. Maybe someone is accusing us of doing something wrong. Or maybe we need to approach a coworker about not meeting a deadline. What can you do to keep difficult conversations from tearing down what you all have worked so hard to build?

It's All in the Attitude and Approach

Moments of truth arise when two or more people have different perceptions of a situation. As you approach what your senses indicate could be a difficult conversation, it's important to remember how your attitude influences the situation. Will you approach the conversation with intent to blame and protect yourself, or will you approach it with the intent to understand?

Often, it is realizing the potential for miscommunication or misunderstanding that makes us sweat before we have a crucial conversation. Acknowledging this possibility is a huge step toward intent to understand. When you walk into a conversation already recognizing there could be reasons for another's behavior that you don't yet see or understand, you are beginning with a healthy approach. If you approach a situation already having determined the other person is at fault, it sets up the conversation for unhealthy conflict.

It's natural for any two people to have a difference of opinion. We may believe a difference of opinion means there is a problem, but sometimes it's not a problem to have conflicting priorities or mismatched goals. There are times when it doesn't really matter. And there are times when varying perspectives can lead to good ideas.

It isn't the fact that we disagree and have conflicts with people at work that is so destructive. The problems come when we have a bad attitude and don't deal with these differences well. If we give ourselves permission to have a good attitude and then learn skills for doing it a different way, we can change the outcome to something positive. Our conscious decision to interact in a healthy way means the discussion can remain productive.

We can prepare to have healthy discussions by becoming aware of our conflict management style and how it impacts our behavior and choices. What is our default response when we encounter disagreement? Do we avoid, compete, compromise, accommodate, or collaborate?

Conflict Management Styles

Many scenarios leading to crucial conversations come about when our perspective or opinion doesn't match someone else's. When faced with such situations, different people respond in different ways. The way you respond is known as your conflict management style. Different conflict management styles fall within a model measuring how much concern you have for yourself (advocacy) and how much concern you have for others (empathy).

None of these styles is inherently bad or good. Some styles lend themselves more than others to the development of understanding and to stronger relationships. In fact, each style can be effective in specific types of situations. It your job to know your own style, to understand which style is appropriate to a given situation, and to recognize which style the other person or people might be using. Understanding and using conflict management styles correctly makes you a good team member.

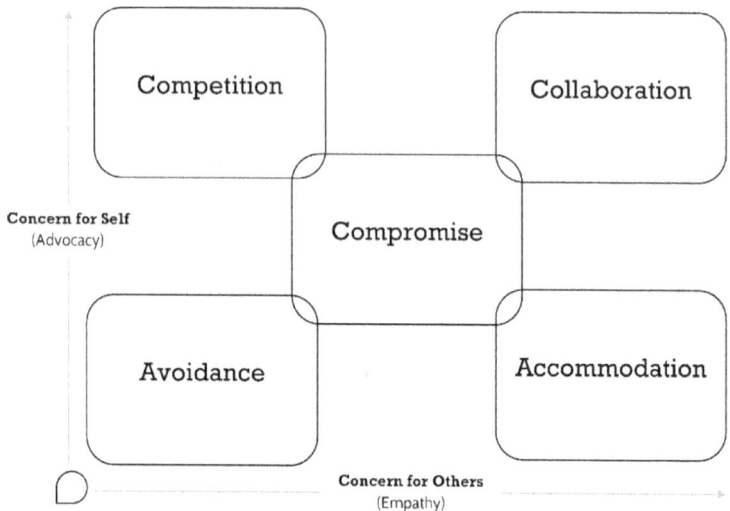

Avoidance: Don't Rock the Boat

When a person approaches a conflict with low concern for self and low concern for others, the result is avoidance. We can use avoidance many ways in a crucial conversation. We might evade the conversation entirely or delegate the confrontation to someone else. Our motive for avoidance might be to not risk hurting someone's feelings, to stay out of trouble, or to buy time.

Avoidance as a primary style is often weak and ineffective, and those who avoid conflict usually seek to blame and protect. When the conflict is trivial or someone else is in a better position to make a decision, avoidance can be an appropriate approach. It also can be a viable option when pressing the issue will cause relationship damage that outweighs the benefits of finding a solution.

Wise team members know you sometimes have to pick your battles. It simply might not be worth engaging in a disagreement about the design of a corporate holiday card. Maybe it's not worth risking a damaging conflict over whether your son wears tennis shoes to a formal occasion. In a scenario when you are ambushed with an issue, initial avoidance can give you time to step back and consider the best approach.

Competition: Forceful Solutions
A person who uses competition as a conflict management style has high concern for self and low concern for others. Competition is a forceful approach to conflict. Conflict competitors often rely on position or influence to press a point of view. It moves you beyond advocating for your own needs to a more forceful position of seeking to win at all costs. People who use a competitive style of conflict management often are motivated to blame and protect.

    A competitive style can be the most effective approach when a crucial conversation requires a quick, firm decision. In an emergency, for an example, there might be little time to discuss differing options and opinions. It might simply be up to you to make a decision to solve the problem now.

    Competition is also effective when the conflict involves a rare, non-negotiable issue for you or your organization. For example, if your coworker is approaching his job in a way that compromises the physical safety of others, little discussion is necessary, even if your coworker fails to see the problem. At times, you may need to use a competitive approach to protect yourself or your company from someone who is trying to manipulate or take advantage of you. If you do have good reasons to take a competitive approach to a conflict, you might need to evaluate the aftermath and debrief with others who felt run-over or used.

Accommodation: Keeping the Peace

When you approach conflict with low concern for self and high concern for others, you are choosing to be accommodating. This approach might seem useful in getting along with others, but even an individual who has the interests of others at heart must be able to assert his own needs and point of view. Accommodation often is chosen by those who value harmony and want to keep the peace or avoid disruption at all costs.

When you accommodate, you can find yourself giving up your position too quickly, even unnecessarily. You might recognize you have misapplied this style if, after a crucial conversation, you harbor feelings of anger or resentment that your position seemed undervalued.

Accommodation is an appropriate approach to conflict when you recognize your perspective or point of view truly is wrong, or the other person truly does have a better idea.

Compromise: No Losers, but No Winners

To compromise means to approach a conflict with moderate concern for self and moderate concern for others. In this style, you press for some of your needs, but give up others. You expect the other party or parties involved do the same. This style is motivated by an intent to understand. Those who use this style are interested in incremental progress, seeking little wins and little concessions. When you choose compromise, no one wins, but no one loses. It's like a tie in a sporting event. Both teams often leave feeling a little disappointed and feeling as though nothing really has been settled.

Compromise is an effective approach to conflict when you're facing time constraints and need a workable solution. If you are facing a complex issue or find yourself in a power struggle, you can use compromise to gain a little positive ground and find a temporary resolution. For example, imagine you are leading a committee tasked with developing a new filing system. Your committee members are in conflict over specific criteria the committee will use to choose a system, but the deadline is fast approaching. You can use compromise to reach a decision quickly or to reach agreement on tabling the decision temporarily during the first phase of the project.

Collaboration: Solutions for Everyone
Approaching conflict with high concern for self and high concern for others is known as collaboration. A person who collaborates looks for solutions that meet his or her needs, as well as the needs of the other party. Collaboration is motivated by an intent to understand. When you use collaboration, you dialogue and problem-solve with others. You are tough about seeking mutually beneficial outcomes. Those who use this style are often relentless in their pursuit of win-win outcomes. Collaboration is about cooperation. It can be the most time-consuming of the conflict styles.

Collaboration is often the best choice when dealing with difficult conversations. When you need to discover and understand another person's perspective, it's important to use this style. Collaboration can also be effective when you need to build trust and agreement by uniting varying points of view. Collaboration is vital when you're facing an important issue as an organization and buy-in is crucial.

Keeping the Conversation Healthy

To be an effective leader, you need to learn how and when to use each conflict management style. You can influence the outcome of any potentially difficult situation by choosing and using the best conflict management style at the right time. The style you choose should be based on your purpose or the objective you want to achieve. Remember to first use facilitation and determine the goal of the crucial conversation.

No matter which style you choose, approaching crucial conversations with the intent to understand the other person and refrain from blame is a healthy place to begin. As you move through the conversation, continue to dialogue using questions, encouraging statements and other techniques of facilitation to keep the conversation on course.

Even when you use all of these techniques, some disagreements might reach a point where they become unhealthy. Feelings are hurt, logic is lost, and positions are taken. What do you do? You might need to deploy alternative methods.

When you notice signs of frustration or anger in yourself or the other person, first slow down the action before the conversation gets any more out of control. Listen carefully to what the other person is saying through both words and body language. Also listen for what is not being said. Instead of interrupting, let the other person vent.

To keep crucial conversations healthy, give the other person the benefit of the doubt. Believe his intentions are good. When you do respond, put yourself on the same side as the other person, with the same goal: to find a solution. Phrase things in terms of "our problem," not "my problem" or "your problem." Avoid using absolute statements, such as "We never do it that way" or "Everyone needs to use this worksheet." Remember healthy conflict can lead to personal and professional growth and better relationships.

At times, a crucial conversation reaches a point of no return, and it's best to end the discussion before permanent damage is done. If this happens to you with a coworker, you could schedule a follow-up meeting and include a third person to serve as a moderator.

Communicating Up

One of the most difficult conversations for some is engaging in a crucial dialogue with the person they report to. This can be unnerving for many reasons. First, the person you report to holds authority over you. She is the one who completes your performance review and decides if you get a raise. She influences your work and your career, and if the conversation goes wrong, it could affect your position.

On the other hand, you want your manager to see you at your best. You want to use this conversation to demonstrate your competence and skill. We all want our managers to believe in us and see our value to the organization. We certainly don't want them to misunderstand our intentions or misconstrue the goal of the conversation. If handled correctly, crucial conversations with managers can have a positive impact on your work, your work relationships, the culture of your department, and the success of the organization.

Why Communicate Up?

Your manager needs you. She needs information and input only you can give because of the work you do every day. You see and experience things she can't experience in the same way. Your perspective is valuable, not only to her, but to the entire organization. When decisions are made without input from employees, details can be forgotten. Your good ideas can't be considered when decision makers don't know about them. Let's say the company's leaders are planning to make big changes. Without your input, they might not have all the information they need to determine all the areas the change will affect.

You've probably heard people say things like leadership is "too far removed from day-to-day operations." Or "management lacks firsthand knowledge of processes." The ongoing conversations you have with your manager help solve this problem. Your conversations help her understand what your day looks like, the challenges you are experiencing, and what's working well. These are all acceptable topics of conversation with your manager, and you actually have a responsibility to share them.

Information from people like you helps companies stay competitive. It helps them look for ways to improve efficiencies, increase customer satisfaction, and stay on the cutting edge. People who are engaged in the daily operation of the organization are best equipped to notice improvements that can help organizations do just that.

Maybe you've tried to share ideas in the past, but felt your ideas weren't considered. It might seem as though your suggestions haven't been welcomed. But that's not necessarily true. Remember, even as you possess information your manager isn't aware of, your manager probably has information you aren't aware of. She sees things from a different perspective, and an idea you share simply might not be perfect at that time, for that situation.

If you've shared your ideas in the past without success, it doesn't mean you shouldn't try again. Consider trying a different approach. See if you get a different response. Even if the answer is no, your initiative is likely to be appreciated.

Do Your Homework

Just like other difficult conversations, you can use a few strategies to help conversations with your manager go more smoothly and be more effective overall. Remember to identify your goal first.

Is it to influence or persuade your manager? Then, you need to build your business case. Frame your ideas in light of how it will impact the team's, department's, or organization's goals.

Take time to do your research. Gather facts to support your idea or opinion. Write down your thoughts and ideas before meeting with your manager. If you don't, there's a good chance you won't remember everything you want to say when you're face-to-face. Your preparation will have a positive effect on your presentation. It shows you've done your homework and the idea is important to you.

Think like your boss. To help her see the issue from your perspective, you also need to see it from her perspective. Is your manager focused on the budget and cutting costs? Explain how the idea will save money. Is she focused on increasing productivity? Explain how your idea will create efficiencies in your area.

Remember Your Goal
As with other difficult conversations, successfully conversing with your manager means first understanding the goal of the conversation. Then, when and if the dialogue seems to be stalling, you must ask facilitative questions that lead toward that goal. What questions could you ask to keep the conversation going? With the skills you are learning, you have some control over this dialogue. You have the ability to create conversations that lead to mutual understanding.

When you've reached an impasse, consider asking questions such as, "Tell me more about your perspective on _____" or "Have you considered the possibility of _____?" Continue using open-ended questions to propel the conversation forward. Stay focused on what you really want. Envision the best case scenario. What will things look like if you are successful in the conversation? The payoff has to be more than proving a point. It has to be more than proving your manager is wrong. An authentic goal stems from integrity.

Sometimes, to understand what you really want, you might need to decide what you don't want. Maybe all you know for now is that you don't want to spark an argument. You don't want to come across as being difficult. Once you define the negative, it will be easier to identify the positive–the results you DO want to work toward.

What do you want for yourself, for your manager, and for others? What would a win-win situation look like? Your facilitative questions will help you uncover what others want. How does that fit with your needs? Any problem has multiple solutions. How can you work together creatively to find a solution that doesn't leave out anyone's needs?

As you are having these crucial conversations, don't forget to monitor your body language and the body language of your manager. Do you see signs that mean you might need to adjust your style? What do you need to focus on to ensure the conversation stays healthy?

Watch for signs that may mean your manager is too busy to discuss the topic in depth. She will appreciate your sensitivity to her needs. Instead of pushing forward right now, ask to schedule a more convenient time. Consider when and where would be the best time to approach this conversation. Should you talk privately, or could the conversation take place during a team meeting?

During the conversation, if you determine either you or your manager needs to gather more information or additional follow-up is needed, set a reasonable time to come back together to continue the discussion. Don't wait for your manager to seek you out, if it is important to you. Demonstrate your belief in the importance of the topic by being the one to seek out your manager.

From a Manager's Perspective
When you don't get the answer you want during the conversation, this doesn't mean your manager didn't hear you. Again, there are always two sides to every situation, and your manager has a different perspective than you. If it's not the right time for your idea, you can use this as an opportunity to learn more about the department's goals and the organization's big picture. Take time to ask for additional insight on the topic to help you understand your manager's perspective.

To nurture your relationship with your manager and set the stage for many successful future conversations, remain open to feedback. Allow yourself to believe your manager has good intentions. She is juggling many different hats. She's human and capable of making mistakes – just like you. Keep an open mind and ask good questions to help you understand her intentions. Then ask for feedback on how your manager believed the conversation went. Even analyzing your conversation skills is an opportunity to learn and grow in your position and your career.

What if your manager shares corrective information relating to your work performance? This is usually a difficult conversation for both of you. For you, it could be a tipping in your career–either positively or negatively. The manner in which you choose to respond to corrective feedback influences your manager's perception of you. Your response says a great deal about your commitment to the organization. It also indicates your level of personal investment in being successful.

Practice not feeling defensive about feedback. Think of it as a gift! Giving you feedback is how managers help you be successful. It's a way to communicate and reinforce expectations, so you can more successfully meet expectations. Feedback provides guidance. Intentionally choose to believe your manager is giving you feedback because she wants you to be successful. Think about it from this perspective: Would you rather your manager didn't tell you if were doing something incorrectly? How would it feel to know you were not performing well, but no one was saying anything to help you improve?

Often, there are gaps between your manager's perspective and your perspective when it comes to your performance. When this happens, focus on specific behaviors rather than focusing on placing blame. Take responsibility for your part in the situation and ask for guidance and help where you need it. Collaborate with your manager to look for strategies that will help you succeed.

The Road to Success: Communication Can Get You There

One of the greatest tools we have in our careers is our ability to communicate well with others. To share our ideas and thoughts. To hear and understand the perspective of others. To truly listen and demonstrate empathy. This all requires a great deal of self-awareness and a conscious effort to behave with intention.

Whether your goal is to climb the ladder, create other opportunities for yourself in the organization, or be the most effective team member in your department, your ability to communicate well is fundamental to your success. Consider how you want to be perceived by others. Do you want the team to view you as helpful and thoughtful? As someone who follows through with their assignments? Do you want your manager to recognize the value you bring to the organization? Effective communication can help you get where you want to be.

Our actions are not always consistent with our intentions. Avoid acting on emotions or impulses. Behave with thoughtful intention. Think about the way others may perceive your actions. Build a habit of asking yourself whether your actions could be misinterpreted by others in any way. Are you sending mixed messages? For example, you may say you are really committed to a new project, but when your part of the project is due, you turn it in a week late. Your actions are not consistent with your intentions. What can you do to match them up?

You have learned how your thoughts become your actions, how body language impacts your messages, and how to ask genuine questions to reach mutual understanding.

You have learned how to successfully navigate conversations. As you can imagine, this is only the beginning. There is so much more you can learn to improve your ability to communicate and to lead. To make these lessons stick, you must continuously reinforce what you've learned. Creating lasting habits takes practice, so continue to practice what you've learned. Continue looking for opportunities to polish your communication skills and add to your knowledge.

Three Things to Remember

1. The way we handle crucial conversations can have a deep impact on the people involved, and on the organization.

2. It is your job to know your own conflict management style, to understand which style is appropriate to a given situation, and to recognize which style the other person or people might be using.

3. Approaching crucial conversations with the intent to understand the other person and refrain from blame is a healthy place to begin.

Putting it to Work

- Write down three valuable ideas from the chapter.

- What one thing can you do to start implementing each idea?

- What impact will taking action have on you or the team you lead?

Chapter 4
Make Time to Manage Time

Time Crunch

The saying goes that work expands to fill the time you have to spend. What do you do when your work overflows your available time? You wouldn't be the only one facing this situation. Managing time is one of the great challenges of the working world.

What does a time-overloaded day look like? The moment you step into your office or work area, it begins. A coworker wants to make a plan for the new project. Before you dig into that, your full inbox needs attention. As you begin working on the emails, your boss texts a request to come to his office. You're worried about what he'll say, but on the way to talk with him, someone hands you an urgent customer request requiring research. Your mind instantly switches gears as you continue walking. How you are going to get that request taken care of today? You barely have enough time to finish the report from last week.

Everyone has days when the workload seems impossible. If you were hired to respond to an ongoing flood of customer questions, this pace is a fact of life for you. For many of us, frantically bouncing from one task to the next has simply become a habit. We focus on completing assignments as they come, instead of being proactive and making a plan. When we're in the middle of one task, we allow ourselves to get sidetracked by another.

Is there anything we can do to stop this uncomfortable rush of activity? Everyone's heard of time management. But it seems like a theory for textbooks, not a practical tool for real people. Is there any real way to become a master of your own time?

Getting Time on Your Side

It's important to control time in the workplace. A disorganized schedule causes stress and makes it hard to focus. Wrestling with time can keep you from thinking as well as you should. Research shows, on really stressful days, workers are 45% less likely to come up with a new idea or solve a problem. Time stress, along with many other stressors, can keep you from being productive—and productivity is the foundation of success.

Let's talk about what it means to be productive. Productivity in an organization is usually measured against your company's ultimate goals. In general, it's a way to determine how well your company is doing. Profit is one measure of productivity, but there are many others. How effective is your customer service program? Maybe your organization measures productivity by the number of conferences attended, new products launched, or connections made in your industry.

Now focus on your team and your own work activities. The productivity of individuals is measured very specifically. Is it your job to process purchase orders? Your boss will probably believe you are productive if you process more requests this week than you did last week. Maybe you are evaluated for productivity based on a quota—the number of repetitive tasks you accomplish in a set amount of time. If you have more flexibility in your job, your productivity might be measured according to how well you meet deadlines.

Being highly productive is more difficult than it seems, because time gets in the way. For one thing, time is hard to measure. In a business, it's easy to measure tangible things, such as land, square footage, equipment, product inventory, and sales. Time is another story. You can't put your hands on it. It looks different to different people. It slips away easily and we often don't even notice. It's tempting to give up on measuring time and just get things done by sheer will.

However, becoming a productive person doesn't happen by sheer will or even by working faster. You may be able to produce more if you work harder, but real productivity happens when you work smarter. Accomplishing a great deal more in your job – increasing your productivity – requires a plan and a change of habits.

Begin by asking yourself, "How can I use my time and other resources to bring the most possible value to my company?" Then, take it one step further. Ask yourself, "What new skills can I develop to help me produce more? How can I become more productive without relying too much on my manager?" If you learn how to manage your time well and increase your productivity independently, you could become one of your company's most valued employees. As a leader, you could help your workgroup become better at managing time.

Time doesn't have to be a burden. You can change the way you think about time. Think of it as a resource you can use to your advantage. First, you must be willing to learn some new skills. Just as you plan your household budget, you have to learn how to budget time. We call it allocating your time – distributing it according to a plan.

The key is the plan. If you learn how to allocate the right amount of time to achieve the right goals at work, this could be the very thing that distinguishes you as an effective employee and leader in your workplace.

The Personal Side of Time

How does a company use time management to reach success? It starts with each individual. Time management is very personal. Managing time well means disciplining yourself, allocating your own time wisely, and gaining control over the outcome of your day.

Tony's Problem:
Tony is not a good time manager. The problem is his big heart. At work, Tony is the person everyone can count on. Even if his workload is heavy, he will almost always stop to help a coworker. One of Tony's problems is an inability to focus on tasks without deadlines. If it has a deadline, especially if the deadline is a priority for someone else, Tony feels motivated to complete the task. If it doesn't have a deadline, no matter how important it is, he can't seem to understand it as a priority. As a result, he is continually engaging in activities that are urgent, but not important.

Someone like Tony can master time management in his personal life, but find himself unable to face the pressure of priorities set by others at work.

Time management is a matter of knowing what you want and having the self-discipline to make it happen. How do you handle time management at home? Do you schedule activities on a calendar hanging on the refrigerator? Maybe your personal schedule is in a calendar application on your phone or laptop. Your routines might include chores, practices, and classes for your kids. You probably go to bed and get up at certain times, so you can make it to your job on time. Successfully managing personal time means allocating time to the activities most important to you or your family.

Now take a step back and take a look at time management in your home from a wider view. Where is most of your time spent? Are any negative habits keeping you from effectively using time? Are your decisions about time supporting the things most important to you?

Even in your personal life, achieving best results means planning, monitoring, and reviewing your plan regularly. If you learn to do it at home, you can take the same skills to work. Maybe you start your workday with a specific plan for doing certain things at certain times. Then, suddenly, other people's priorities change your plan or completely destroy it. This often happens when people react to events without doing any planning.

Tony's style of time management is reactive. He responds to what's happening right now around him. He can't seem to clearly decide how his day should go, and then stick to the plan. Some people are just stubborn. They refuse to make themselves stop to think ahead. Instead, they simply react to what others bring their way. We've all responded reactively on some level. We may not have realized neglecting to manage our time leads to many lost opportunities.

What if you took a different approach? The opposite of reactivity is proactivity. Proactive people don't just wait for things to happen. They make things happen through decisions and actions. Proactive time managers take time to look ahead – to anticipate change and formulate plans for the team that shape the future. How could becoming more proactive help Tony?

Tony's Solution:
With a little guidance, Tony learns the difference between urgency and priority. Now, he handles interruptions from his coworkers much better. He hasn't given up helping; he simply has learned to analyze each request according to the plan - his plan, his team's plan, or the company's plan. Each time a coworker asks him to help, he first asks questions about the importance of the task. When he understands more, he chooses a way to respond. Sometimes, he gives advice immediately. Sometimes, he asks for more information. Often, it's best to schedule a time to discuss the issue later. Tony is still known as the person everyone can count on.

Tony has learned some interesting skills to control the amount of time impromptu conversations steal from his day:

- When someone comes into his office, he limits unscheduled conversations by standing and moving to the front of his desk. This is a nonverbal message that the interaction needs to be short.
- Rather than trying to solve the problem on the spot, Tony has learned to create a temporary plan. He might ask for extra time to consider the idea, and then get back to his coworker with well-thought-out ideas.
- He has learned to be honest about his time. He might say something like, "I like that idea. May we talk about it more when I can give it my full attention? What about this afternoon?"

Time's Wasting Away

Joan and Brent are assigned to scan boxes of paper order forms and convert them to digital files within the next two weeks. They decide to split the job, each taking half of the files. Both have full inboxes already, and they know it will be a challenge to complete the filing job on top of everything else.

Brent begins working immediately. He works for about 15 minutes, then stops. Every day, he works another 15 minutes. Joan smiles to herself. There is plenty of time left before the deadline, and she believes Brent is wasting time overall every time he switches gears to the filing project and back. Her strategy is to first complete the pressing work in her inbox. Then, the last few days of the two weeks, she will scan all the files at once. She watches Brent work for a minute, then gets herself a cup of coffee and relaxes into her daily work.

At the end of two weeks, Joan is scrambling to finish the file scans, and still has an inbox piled with work. Brent is moving on to the next project. What went wrong? When Joan looks at her timesheet, she finds the problem. She thought there was plenty of time left to get the file scanning done, so she took more time than necessary to do other tasks. She has to admit Brent's approach was better in this case.

It's easy to waste time at work. It happens almost without us realizing it, even when we have the best intentions. Time often slips away in small increments that add up faster than we realize. The total amount of time lost can have a real impact on the company. Every hour of your time at work is worth a certain number of dollars. If you are paid hourly, the value of an hour of work is your hourly wage. If you are salaried, simply divide your salary by the number of hours worked to come up with the value of one hour of your work.

Let's look at Joan's work schedule. She estimates an average of three times a day when she could be wasting time in 15-minute increments: 1) leisurely conversing with coworkers several times during the day, 2) figuring out which projects to work on each day, 3) stopping work to review email or take phone calls. If there are 22 work days in a month, this adds up to 16 ½ hours of wasted time. Joan's wage is $12 per hour.

At first, this doesn't sound like much. Then we remember it's only one month. And Joan is only one employee. The following chart shows how wasted time can add up quickly for a company and affect its bottom line. The numbers in the chart are based on a 40-hour week and a conservative estimate of 12 hours of wasted time per month.

The Cost of Time-Wasters

Annual Salary	Monthly Waste	Annual Waste	x 10 Employees
$25,000	$144.23	$1,730.77	$17,307.70
$45,000	$259.62	$3,115.38	$31,153.80
$65,000	$375.00	$4,500.00	$45,000.00
$85,000	$490.38	$5,884.62	$58,846.20

This chart reflects only small increments of time wasted. What about larger instances of wasted time? A comprehensive time study in your company would probably reveal many projects, tasks, and actions that aren't really adding to the company's value. What if you could identify some of these wasted activities and consciously choose to do something more productive instead? What if all the employees in your organization did this? Imagine how much more productive you all could be! As Benjamin Franklin said, "Time is money!"

Eliminating nonproductive activities is one of the best time management tools available to you. Once you remove the waste, it's easier to identify priorities. It not only makes you a better employee, but it can lead your company to greater success.

In your workplace, what kinds of activities could be considered time wasters? Here are a few common causes of low productivity:

- Procrastination and indecision
- Stress and fatigue
- Inability to say "no"
- Personal disorganization
- Interruptions (visitors, phone calls, emails, texts)
- Unclear communication
- Unnecessary meetings
- Un-delegated tasks
- Working with incomplete information
- Crisis management
- Inadequate technical knowledge
- Unclear objectives and priorities
- Lack of planning
- Social media
- Tinkering with technology

What is the consequence of spending time on nonproductive activities? It hobbles your ability to be successful, and your company's. It also reduces the profitability of the organization, which affects your job and everyone else's. Time can be a great asset when you use it correctly, and it can be your worst enemy when you waste it. Becoming aware of the potential for wasted time is one of the first steps toward managing time well.

Where Has the Time Gone?

Now you know the great value of your time at work. Don't you wonder how much time you actually are wasting? What if you could figure out where your time is slipping away? How much could you increase your productivity? Understanding this is an important aspect of time management. If you don't know where your time is going, you can't manage it better.

The best way to uncover the secrets of your time is to monitor yourself for a while through a personal time study. Look at the following activity log sheet. This is a format used by many companies to analyze time. Employees carry one of these activity logs with them throughout the day, making marks to represent each activity they engage in.

Activity Log: Tuesday

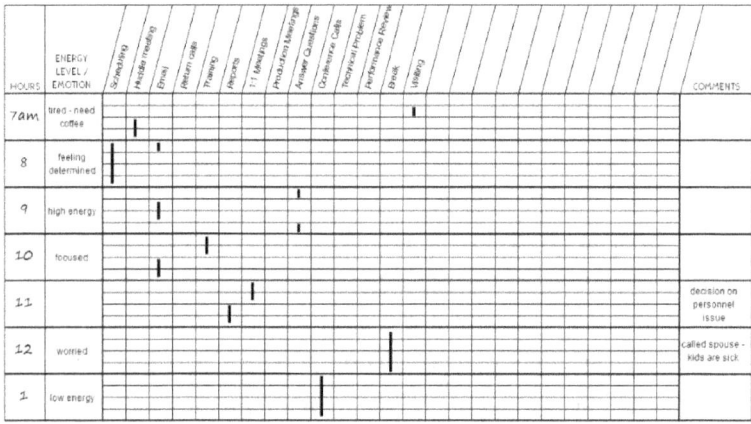

The activity log will help only if you're honest and faithful about logging the details. As you can see, you not only log the time, but you also make notes about your energy level and emotions. Later, this can help you plan for the most challenging or most important work during hours when you're feeling the most energetic. Many people find they have a consistent downswing in energy later in the afternoon. This is a good time to schedule low-energy tasks, routine work, or physical activity (to help you wake up).

If it's difficult to remember to log your time, try setting a timer for 45 minutes. When the timer goes off, think back to the tasks you completed during that time and enter them on the log. If you wait till the end of the day to complete your log, it will likely be too difficult to remember details. And it's the details that are important!

Keep a daily log for a few weeks. Once you have accumulated a stack of timesheets, analyze the way you've spent your time. Notice any habits stealing time from your day? How much time do you spend talking with other people? Are meetings taking too long? Are computer problems keeping you from working efficiently? When is it easiest for you to concentrate?

With a highlighter, color entries in the activity log representing any times you would consider to be wasted time. How much color do you see on your log sheets? You might be shocked! Time wasters sneak into our schedules very easily. Time-wasting activities are sometimes very good at camouflaging themselves. It can seem as though an activity is productive, just because you're not sitting still in your chair. This exercise is designed to reveal all your time wasters. Your logs will make it possible to regain those hours for more productive work.

Remember, this exercise works only if you complete it fully. To be honest, it can be difficult to sustain the effort, so prepare yourself. Then, remind yourself the effort is worthwhile and you won't be doing it forever. The potential payoff at the end of the exercise is increased productivity. Your hard work could lead to recognition for you and greater opportunities for your company.

Productivity is More than a Numbers Game

If you do more things in less time, does that make you more productive? Not necessarily. A better gauge of productivity is each task's eventual impact. A seemingly insignificant task might actually make a big difference a year down the road. A lengthy task with a lot of steps might actually lead to no substantial gain for anyone.

The activity log uncovers tasks you may be able to eliminate from your day. It gives you more hours to work with. How will you spend that time? You've worked hard to free up those hours, so you should use the time wisely. We call tasks that make the biggest impact on an organization High Payoff Activities (HPAs).

Many HPAs don't lead to immediate, tangible benefits, such as increased sales or new customers. Instead, they provide value by paving the way for greater growth or better performance. Training and coaching are high payoff activities that prepare a workforce to perform more effectively. Some HPAs help strengthen the infrastructure of your company. This includes planning, creating systems, and acquiring equipment and tools. What about tasks that make your systems run more smoothly? These HPAs might include status reports, maintenance, and new product research.

Every person and every company has different HPAs. The only way to identify your HPAs is to know the ultimate goals you're working toward. Reaching the goal is the ultimate payoff.

The Ultimate Payoff

Why do you go to work every day? It's obvious, isn't it? You work to make money. What will you do with your money? You probably buy necessities. You also likely save for important things like vacation, retirement, and your children's education. So, money isn't your goal at all! What you need and want in your life–those are the reasons you get up every morning and go to work.

Many studies show reaching for specific goals motivates people and helps them focus. When you have goals, you know what to do next. You don't waste time wondering. To be productive and manage your time well, you need to know where you're headed.

A famous study of goals was conducted at Harvard business school in 1979. The study asked the question, "Have you set clear, written goals for your future and made plans to accomplish them?" Only 3% of the graduates had written down their goals and plans. Thirteen percent did have goals, but they hadn't written them down. Eighty-four percent had no goals at all. Ten years later, the same people were interviewed, with these stunning results: those who wrote down their goals were earning an average of 10 times as much as the other 97% put together! Just writing down the goal made that much difference. That's how powerful goals can be.

Which ultimate goals motivate you at work?
In the workplace, organizational and department goals provide a target for everyone to focus on. Departments align their goals to fit within the corporate goals. Individuals align personal goals to fit within the department. This creates a framework to help you choose what to spend your time on. Goal-backed activities will take you where you want to go, faster, and more efficiently.

Goals can't be too general or vague. Setting undefined goals is a little like plotting a route to California from Nebraska without knowing which town you're going to. You can't just say you're going to California. Which highway would you take? To plot an efficient route, you have to know whether you're headed toward San Francisco in the north or San Diego in the south. It works the same with goals at work–they need to be well-defined.

Think of your organization's goals as final destinations. Do you know what they are in your organization? If you don't, ask your manager. Talk about ways your work impacts the goals of the corporation and the department. Then carefully choose your own priorities and formulate individual goals.

The most effective goals have certain qualities in common that make them work. These qualities follow the acronym "SMART."

SMART Goals Are:
- **S**pecific, so the goal setter knows exactly what to work toward.
- **M**easurable, so you know when you've reached your goal.
- **A**ction-oriented, so you know exactly what to do.
- **R**ealistic, so you believe you can actually reach your goal.
- **T**imely, to create a sense of urgency.

Defining your goals in this way gives you a clear destination. A SMART goal helps you and your team make better use of your time and become more productive.

Make Time to Plan

Moving toward your goals without a plan leads to wasted time and lost productivity. Planning takes a little time, but it can save time in the end. We sometimes believe planning isn't urgent–that it's an option. Once we experience the power of planning, we can see what a difference it makes, and we realize it's not an option. Planning is a critical tool for mastering time management.

An action plan helps you and your team match your work to the company's objectives, then move forward confidently to reach them. It helps you identify both short-term and long-term goals to reach those ultimate objectives.

At work, you can't plan without considering the entire team. However, once you've established the needs of the group, then it's your responsibility to assemble a coordinating personal plan. Work with your manager to write down your goals. Then create timelines for carrying them out. Create a process that works for you to list tasks, schedule activities, and track achievements.

So, you've created a plan. Do you think you're finished? You're not! Planning is an ongoing process. To be successful, you have to regularly review the steps of the plan. Every plan has to be revised mid-stream to adapt to new circumstances and take advantage of new ideas. This brings up another important aspect of planning. What's the best way to determine exactly what those steps should be toward a goal?

Many people use a process called "backwards planning." It begins with your end goal. To backwards plan, you list the final deadline, then work backwards, adding steps until you reach today. Think of each step and estimate how long it will take. You might need to experiment and adjust dates to fit the time interval between now and the goal.

Backwards planning is a great way to make sure you include every action, resource, and sub-goal necessary to reach your goal. It also helps ensure you don't run out of time.

Steps to Backwards Planning

1. Make a list of tasks you must complete to achieve the desired result.
2. Using a calendar, begin by listing the last task you expect to occur before the final product is produced or the event takes place.
3. Consider all of that task's components. If component tasks need to be completed by specific dates, work backwards from those dates and write them on your calendar as well.

4. Continue with the next-to-last task, and so on, until you have worked up to the most immediate task.
5. If other teams or team members are involved or affected, work with them to agree on the tasks and deadlines.

Here's how backwards planning looks when it's completed:

Task	Owner	Deadline	Week 1 Aug 18-22	Week 2 Aug 25-29	Week 3 Sept 1-5	Week 4 Sept 8-12	Week 5 Sep 15-19	Retreat Sep 23-24
Prepare agenda	Cheryl	Aug 19	■					
Set budget	Brian	Aug 21	■					
Reserve rooms	Liz	Aug 26		■				
Create event and invite department	Cheryl	Aug 28		■				
Prepare content	Cheryl	Sep 10			■	■		
Arrange food	Liz	Sep 12				■		
Print materials	Liz	Sep 20					■	

No matter what method you use to plan, writing down the steps helps you focus your work. It gives you and your workgroup a clear path to follow, so no one will waste time. Best of all for those of us who tend to procrastinate, planning keeps us on track and makes it clear what we should do next.

Use a Planning System

How can you put your plan into action? What should you do today? How should you prepare for upcoming steps? In addition to your plan's steps, you will encounter many related thoughts, ideas, and facts you need to process every day. You may have ideas for the new telephone system that you don't want to forget to tell your manager. Maybe you have questions for the software trainer or you've run across facts to use in a presentation. To capture it all, you need a planning system!

You should choose a personal planning system that fits you best. What format is the easiest for you to access from your workstation? Some people need a paper planner to carry with them. Some choose an electronic system to keep their desks clear. Computer or online systems provide helpful features, such as instant report creation and automatic numerical or alphabetical ordering. You may want to experiment in the beginning to see what you like. Eventually, it's important to pick one method and stay with it.

Plan Time to Plan
Your goals are clear and your plan is in place. You've neatly written today's agenda in the pages of your planner. Everything looks so nice, and it feels good to have done the work to reach this point. When you close the cover of your planner, remind yourself you must open it up often to refer back to the plan. Goals and plans are not just ideas. They are tools to be continually revisited, reviewed, and revised. You should open your planner every day to add new tasks, check next steps, record details, and capture ideas.

To make sure your planner doesn't end up lost in the back of a drawer, schedule planning time at the end of every day. Allow yourself to take satisfaction in completing tasks and checking them off. If you haven't completed all of today's tasks, carry them over to tomorrow's page. Write down thoughts you want to remember to tell the team.

At the end of each week, it's time for FAC – 15 minutes of Friday Afternoon Calendaring. Look back at the week's pages in your planner. How did you do? What's left to do? Add leftover tasks to the next week and schedule what you can. Think about your goals and plans. Is this still the right direction? Talk with your manager about any adjustments you need to make. Doesn't this feel good? You get to consciously close out the week. Your efforts to plan give you peace of mind to enjoy your weekend.

The more you work with your planning system, the better you will get to know it. You'll discover the most efficient ways to record your goals, anticipate next steps, schedule meetings, check off tasks, and share your plan with others (including your boss) to save time and coordinate efforts. You'll begin to see patterns in your work style and make adjustments. You'll learn to gracefully refocus to accommodate interruptions and major changes in project direction.

Categorizing and Prioritizing

Allison looked at the list of steps in her project plan. It was overwhelming. How could she possibly get all of it done? "It's not humanly possible," she thought, realizing at least a few items on the list realistically would never get done. She decided she might as well admit she couldn't do everything. Now, she has to figure out which important tasks to keep and which tasks to abandon. Before she can begin working, she needs to prioritize.

Prioritizing tasks is a critical time management skill. If we don't identify what needs to be done first, we are simply randomly performing tasks that may or may not take us efficiently toward our goals. Not prioritizing is another way to waste time!

What's the best way to decide which tasks are more important than others? Begin by categorizing the tasks on your list. Try ranking them by the importance of their impact on your goals. Tasks with the greatest impact go at the top of your list. You might begin by categorizing the tasks. Separate them into three categories by marking them with an A, B, or C:

- A   Critical tasks
- B   Important, but not critical tasks
- C   Less important tasks

Now, decide how you will manage these tasks based on order of priority. Handle critical tasks first to make sure they get done. You may have to schedule critical tasks later in the day if you have to wait for equipment or personnel. While you wait, complete category B tasks. Less important tasks are often less time-consuming. Insert Category C tasks at any time to give you a break. How else might you organize your priorities? If two tasks are equal in importance, consider doing the one you dread first to get it over with.

	URGENT	NOT URGENT
IMPORTANT	I.	II.
NOT IMPORTANT	III.	IV.

Keep in mind some activities are urgent because they are time sensitive. Some are urgent because they address emergency situations. Other activities are not urgent, but they do have a high level of importance. Important activities may have the greatest impact over the long-term. A task might be considered important because it's meaningful to the company owner. It can sometimes be difficult to decide whether to complete urgent or important tasks first. Activities that are both urgent and important should be done before anything else.

Master Time Managers

Are you beginning to see how all the pieces of time management fit together? One step at a time, you are acquiring skills and ideas to help you become more efficient and productive. You can help your coworkers gain some of the same skills. At the very least, make their lives easier and help them be more productive by keeping them updated on your progress. Schedule regular reports to show you value their contributions.

An effective leader thinks beyond herself and her personal goals. She looks for ways to connect all members of the team-to streamline communication, planning, and time management. How can you help others make good decisions? How can you help them feel confident about their ability to plan? It could be as simple as providing verbal encouragement. Maybe you offer to spend an hour with a colleague fine-tuning ways to use his planner more effectively.

Leaders use coordinated planning and time management to help teams work better and faster. It's up to a leader to send agendas, assignments, reminders, schedules, and other tools to keep things moving. Leaders help team members stay focused on the greater goals.

There are only 24 hours in the day. How can you use them like a master time manager?

Three Things to Remember

1. Managing time well is about disciplining yourself, allocating your own time wisely, and gaining control over the outcome of your day.

2. Moving toward your goals without a plan leads to wasted time and lost productivity.

3. Proactive time managers take time to look ahead – to anticipate change and formulate plans that shape the future.

Putting it to Work

- Write down three valuable ideas from the chapter.

- What one thing can you do to start implementing each idea?

- What impact will taking action have on you or the team you lead?

Chapter 5
Opportunities to Lead

Stepping Into Leadership

Influence, communication, time management—in the past few lessons, you've picked up valuable knowledge about some of the most important leadership skills. If you continue practicing the principles you've learned, your leadership abilities will grow; and when an opportunity for leading comes along, you'll be ready!

Don't worry if you feel you still have a lot to learn. It will come. The truth is, we all continue to learn. In fact, you should make it a point to never stop learning. The best leaders are always looking for new ways to sharpen their skills and become better at what they do. The alternative is to stop growing. If you stop learning, you are saying "No" to possibilities.

As your leadership skills develop, you will begin noticing opportunities within your organization - and your life - to use what you've learned. Before you took this course, you might not even have noticed situations that needed you to lead. You might not have considered yourself to be a person who can take things in hand and get things done.

What kinds of things happen in an organization that call for a leader? Look around and begin listening to conversations people are having. Take time to notice what's happening. How are people interacting? You might be assigned to lead a group or act as a mentor to a new employee. Maybe you'll see an opportunity and volunteer to manage the efforts of a group, especially if the objectives of the project fit your interest and skills.

What kinds of situations could you find yourself in as a leader? What difficulties are you likely to face? Let's take a look at some common leadership opportunities and challenges you might encounter.

Leading Is More Than Doing

Hector is a department manager in a local corporation. He's been at work for only a short time, but he's already frustrated with the behavior of his direct reports today. Slumping in his chair, he mutters under his breath, "I don't get it! Why aren't we making progress on the new software initiative?"

What's the problem here?
Is Hector's team made of lazy, unskilled, and irresponsible people? No. He leads a team of skilled, competent people who have been successful in the past. So, what explains the lack of progress?

Hector decides to talk with his employees one-on-one, and he soon discovers a pattern. Each employee tells a variation of the same story:

> *"I've offered to help Kim. I wanted to be part of making this process work. I've given her ideas and suggestions, but Kim wants to control everything and doesn't take any suggestions. She pretty much makes all the decisions and won't let me help."*

Kim is the project manager on the software initiative. As Hector finds out through Kim's coworkers, Kim feels as though she has to do it all. She keeps a tight rein on the group, answers all their questions, fixes all their problems, and makes all the decisions. When it comes to doing the actual work, she gives her team members small tasks to complete, but keeps the most important work for herself.

Sharing responsibilities isn't something Kim likes to do. In fact, she fears it. After all, if she is going to be held accountable for getting the work done, why should she risk transferring tasks to people whose skills are not on par with hers? Kim is too busy to spend time teaching others and following up on their work. To her, sharing the responsibility just doesn't make sense.

Kim most likely started in this role with good intentions. Then, for some reason she became unable or unwilling to delegate and share responsibilities. She probably doesn't realize the devastating consequences of taking on all of the work herself.

Kim is spending all of her time on this project, and the rest of her responsibilities are suffering, even though she's working extra hours. Because Kim hasn't asked the other implementation team members for input, the modules she created aren't working. The others have become disengaged from the project. Kim has trained them not to help – and not to care.

Reluctance to Share Responsibility

It's not unusual to find professionals, like Kim, who are uncomfortable with and even fearful of delegating or sharing responsibility for certain projects. How did this happen to Kim? Maybe she tried to get others involved, but felt burned when a task wasn't completed correctly. Maybe she failed to understand that the knowledge and skills of other team members are critical to effectively implement the project. Most teams are assembled because there's a need for a variety of perspectives, talents, and skills. There's a benefit to having a project completed by a team. Leading means getting work done through the activity of others.

Maybe Kim knows all this, but was simply unprepared to lead a project. When new leaders find themselves uncomfortable with leading, they sometimes return to a focus on the individual production skills that made them successful in the past. It's what they are comfortable with. It may seem easier than taking on something new: sharing responsibility.

It's easy to find excuses to avoid sharing responsibility. Maybe this has happened to you. Did you believe you can do a task better and faster than anyone else? Maybe you thought it would be better for you to do it rather than someone with lesser skills. Maybe you enjoyed the work and didn't want to let it go. Was your schedule too busy to train someone else?

You might have a long list of other reasons to avoid sharing responsibility, such as:

- You're unsure what to share or delegate.
- You're unsure when to share or delegate.
- You're unsure how to share or delegate.
- You fear other employees will resent you.
- You lack confidence in your team members.
- You fear loss of power and control.
- You're unwilling to let members make decisions and be held accountable for those decisions.
- You're uncomfortable with training or teaching others.
- You feel possessive of a project.
- You feel guilty because your team members are already busy.

Leaders and team members alike must move past these excuses. There's too much at stake not to! What good does it do if you burn out, relationships are damaged, and deadlines are jeopardized? Almost always, those who insist on doing all the work have good intentions. They believe they're doing what's best for the project or giving the other team members a break. In spite of good intentions, though, projects always work better when the talents of the entire team are used to their fullest.

Sharing responsibility is an important aspect of being an effective team member. For the individual, it's an essential part of achieving personal growth. Sharing responsibilities ensures no one carries too much of the burden. It also helps team members bond, builds loyalty, and uncovers powerful opportunities for collaboration. For an organization, well-balanced workgroups are critical. Success depends upon everyone's ability to coordinate skills and tasks – to get things done, meet schedules, and fulfill production expectations. In short, sharing responsibility is essential!

Managing Projects

From time to time, whether you are assigned or you initiate it, you may be called upon to manage or champion a project. What does this mean? It means you've been put in a position to be responsible. It's up to you to gather the resources, create a plan, and make sure the project is completed. This doesn't necessarily mean you do all of the steps to complete the project. The responsibility you've been given might include pulling together coworkers and members of different teams.

In this role, what kinds of tasks will you be completing? Here are just a few possibilities:

- Determine the project goals.
- Research the project background.
- Put a project plan together.
- Assign tasks and responsibilities to co-workers.
- Establish deadlines and due dates.
- Keep the team informed of progress.

- Remind team members of upcoming dates and meetings.
- Report to your manager.

You can use leadership skills to fulfill these responsibilities. When you serve in a project leader role or any other kind of leadership role, formal or informal, you must communicate. You can use your influence to persuade, organize, and guide people. You can help the team manage time. Leaders take initiative, pull resources together, and encourage their colleagues to stay focused on the goal.

If everything goes smoothly, you will feel a great sense of accomplishment. On the way to success, however, you may find you have to go over a few bumps. Very few project teams can boast zero issues! It's a good thing you've learned how to conduct difficult conversations. Your responsibilities include finding ways to help your team members with their struggles.

For example, sometimes team members miss deadlines or can't attend scheduled meetings. What's your initial reaction? You may believe they are being lazy. It might seem as though they don't care about the project and their responsibilities. As the project leader, you might feel you have a right to be angry about this. It's tempting to take it personally.

When this happens, take a step back and breathe. Resist the urge to retaliate or to keep score. Begin by thinking about the issue from the other person's point of view. You probably have been in a similar situation. How did you feel when something like this happened to you? Think back to a time when you missed a meeting. What was the reason? Did you do it just to cause trouble? Probably not!

In most cases, when someone misses a meeting or fails to live up to a responsibility, there's a reason. It's very unlikely they don't care. Even people who have a tendency toward laziness don't want to be left out. Rather than assuming the person is being difficult on purpose, look at this as a perfect time to call or meet and talk with them about it. Find out how you can help make things better.

This is the time to believe your coworkers and team members are trying to do the right thing. You can choose to believe they have good intentions. And then you can help them find ways to remove the barriers so all of you can be successful.

Make No Excuses, Tell No Lies

The pace of business is fast! As technology has advanced, we thought it was going to give us more leisure time. Instead, now businesses want to do more and more all the time, using technology to speed up productivity. As a result, employees at all levels are increasingly expected to do more with less. That makes time a precious commodity.

Most of us have long to-do lists. Sometimes it's hard to get everything done. How does your task list look at the end of the day? On many days, you may find several items you didn't get to. You aren't alone! Did you try to do too much? Maybe it was impossible to get that many things done in one day. Maybe you had too many interruptions, or maybe you could have planned better. What other reasons could there be?

The To-Do List as a Form of Torture
Forbes business writer Vanessa Loder likens a long to-do list to torture. When you know you can't get everything done on your list, it puts continual pressure on you from the time you start your day to the time you go home at night. It sets you up to fail and wastes a ton of energy.

Her advice is to keep your list simple. Be realistic. On your list, include only items you truly believe you can accomplish. Loder suggests listing no more than three items per day. If it's too hard to do that, she recommends writing down everything else you're thinking about on a separate list, then setting that list aside.

Sometimes it's tempting to make excuses for things that didn't get done. If we think we're going to be in big trouble, we might look for something on which to blame our lack of performance. It's human nature to make mistakes, but we should do everything we can to accomplish our goals. It's important to keep looking for ways to fulfill the promises we make.

When things go wrong, the only way to find proper solutions is to be honest. As a leader, you can model this behavior for your team members. Show them your team is a place where they won't be penalized for honesty. Blame is unproductive. Create a working environment where everyone is looking forward to solutions, rather than looking back and dwelling on problems.

Encourage your colleagues to think about the reasons your team encountered a problem. This type of looking backward is productive. Analyze the steps and look for clues. What went wrong? Where did the chain of productivity break? Is it something that can be fixed with a few adjustments? Or was it just an unfortunate circumstance?

One common reason tasks go undone is conflicting priorities. When a number of people have to work together to accomplish a project, it can be very difficult to coordinate and agree on schedules and deadlines. Even when a group works together to create a plan, differing responsibilities can sometimes clash.

Conflicting priorities show up in different ways. Many times, priorities from another person or another group take precedence over your project. A crisis, personal or professional, is often a priority that keeps team members from living up to responsibilities. A request from a customer or a company executive usually supersedes the needs of an internal committee.

No matter what the reason for conflicting priorities, as the leader of the group, you must deal with the fact that an expectation wasn't met. You need to uncover any problems and find solutions in order for the project to move ahead.

How can you find out exactly what happened? What needs to happen now to fix the problem? You can use your communications skills to do some fact-finding. Again, it's important to approach it from a position of believing the other person has good intentions.

Shelley is a member of your safety team. She was assigned the task of gathering information from all departments. Along with other members of the team, Shelley helped create a plan, including scheduled deadlines. The deadline for delivery of her information was yesterday. Other project members have turned in their information, but Shelley's is missing. As the project lead, it's your responsibility to find out what happened and fix the problem. Your ultimate goal is to get the project moving again, because your company has safety regulations to meet.

How did you find out Shelley would not meet the deadline? When an expectation won't be met, it's always best to find out sooner rather than later. A heads-up on any difficulties allows you to successfully make adjustments to the plan. If there's a crisis, you may not be able to control when you learn about the lapse in responsibility. Barring a crisis, you should make it clear to your team that you need to know about problems as soon as possible. You may still have a coworker who waits until the last minute to inform you of a problem. When this happens, you need to address it promptly, so it won't happen again.

The best way to address a difficult issue like this is to schedule a face-to-face discussion. This is not the time to use email or texting. Remember to assume Shelley had good intentions. There must be a reason she was unable to meet expectations.

Use the steps of The Conversation to help you organize your thoughts. As we learned in a previous lesson, The Conversation gives you an opportunity to gather information without making assumptions. It invites the other person to participate in finding a solution. It helps you work together on a plan to move forward.

Your conversation with Shelley might go something like this:

- **You:** Shelley, may I talk to you about the information you were going to send me for the safety project? I need some help.

- **Shelley:** Sure. What do you need?

- **You:** The last I knew, we agreed you'd send me the information for the safety project by the end of yesterday. But I didn't hear you weren't going to be able to send it until after I thought I was going to get it. Can you help me understand what happened?

- **Shelley:** Sorry about that! I was working on it the day before and had a good start, but I got stuck. Then I got busy yesterday doing other things. My boss wanted me to take care of a last-minute project for her, and it took all day.

- **You:** I understand. It's difficult when other priorities interfere. Can I ask you to do something in the future?

- **Shelley:** Sure. What's that?

- **You:** Next time, if there's a point when you think you're not going to be able to get information to me or you get stuck, will you let me know as soon as you can? I might be able to do something to help you, or I could find another way to get the information. I know you were working on it, and I'm not angry. It did put me behind on the things I needed to do, and it might make it more difficult to reach the deadline. If I had known, we could've come up with a plan B.

- **Shelley:** That makes sense. I will try to remember to do that in the future. Maybe we also could build in some checkpoints in the schedule, to make sure everyone is on track.

- **You:** That's a great idea! Thanks. Do you have a minute to talk about how we might adjust the schedule now?

In this conversation, you're simply asking that Shelley keep you informed. You have assumed she had good intentions, and she did. You stayed respectful and collaborative. You reminded her of what she agreed to do and you clarified the problem you noticed. You asked for help understanding the problem, instead of getting angry and blaming her. For that reason, she didn't feel defensive. She was willing to be honest and she didn't make excuses. She explained what happened and you were able to respond with a solution. She even offered an additional solution of her own.

When you are addressing problems with your coworkers, the focus should always be on finding ways to meet the project goals. This takes the focus off of the other person's shortcomings, gives your colleague encouragement for her ongoing work, and prevents the relationship from being damaged. After a conversation like the one above between you and Shelley, people often feel even more appreciative of one another. It's this kind of successful interaction that helps team members work well together– and enjoy their work!

Don't forget, at the end of a conversation like this, it's a very important to agree on a plan of action going forward. This helps everyone avoid making the same mistake again. It also reinforces for all members of the team that communication is critical. When something goes wrong next time, they won't be afraid to be honest. They'll all know they need to stop and make adjustments. When you asked Shelley to keep you in the loop, you were simply asking for her help. As a responsible coworker, you should demonstrate the same courtesy and keep her in the loop, too.

Do Give Me That Attitude!

Luckily, even though your discussion with Shelley was difficult, she had a great attitude. So did you. That's probably one of the reasons the conversation went well.

Is this the way conversations go where you work? In many organizations, there are a few people who have bad attitudes most of the time, and that can make it difficult to solve problems. Everyone has bad days and can find themselves having a bad attitude. You might have noticed, in many tense situations within the workplace, one of the biggest problems is attitude.

What is attitude? It's hard to define exactly what the word means. First of all, attitude is a state of mind that reflects the way you're feeling. Attitude can be good or bad, positive or negative.

Sometimes we say people have "an attitude." We mean they have a chip on their shoulder.

People's attitudes usually show up in their behavior. Think about the people you appreciate and look up to. Do they make excuses and assume things won't improve? Or are they usually looking for ways to make things better? Do they complain about a lot of things, or do they tend to smile and laugh? How do they handle difficult situations and bad days?

When someone has a good attitude...
...we describe them as happy and enjoyable to be around. People with good attitudes focus on the positive. Some people have good attitudes most of the time. Even when they have difficult days, they try to find solutions to problems, rather than complaining. They aren't afraid to ask for help, and they're willing to give their colleagues help when needed.

When someone has a bad attitude...
...we describe them as grouchy and no fun to be around. People with bad attitudes focus on the negative. Some people have bad attitudes most of the time. A difficult day just seems to fuel their anger and frustration. Even when someone tries to cheer them up, they can't to find it within themselves to turn things around. They keep to themselves, wallow in their misery, and seem to enjoy feeling bad.

Every day, there will be things that don't go the way you want them to and you will be faced with difficult circumstances. You get to choose how you will respond. You can choose to get caught up in the negativity of the situation, or you can choose to have a good attitude, emphasize the positive and find a way to make things better.

It can be difficult to lead a team with members who make excuses and have bad attitudes. You'll have plenty of opportunities to use your difficult conversation skills! Take time to understand what's causing the problems and show respect for your team members. When you handle the situation calmly and thoughtfully, they may even find it difficult to keep having a bad attitude.

One of the most effective ways to turn around the attitudes and behaviors of your colleagues is to model good attitudes and effective communication skills. As you learn more about being a leader and begin to act the part, people will notice. They will pick up good habits from you.

What are some of the skills, attitudes, and behaviors your colleagues might pick up from you? A number of consistent qualities have been attributed to leaders over the ages. Here are just a few of the most important ones:

Leaders are:
- Visionary (they look ahead).
- Proactive (they don't use problems as an excuse).
- Problem-solvers (they never complain and they have options).
- People-centered (they enjoy people and are always willing to help).

What if you were to turn some of these qualities into habits in your personal quest to become a good leader? It's a proven fact that people influence each other. You could inspire your colleagues to raise their standards. How might this change them for the better?

Imagine a team consisting of workers like this:
- Jake is always willing to pitch in and help, even when it's not really his job.
- Emily never complains. If there is a problem, she immediately comes up with options that might work.
- Sara always takes responsibility for her actions, instead of blaming other people or departments. She works to find a solution, rather than finding fault.
- Eli has had a rough life and a lot of family issues, but he never uses this as an excuse to stop him from getting the job done.

When you encourage your colleagues to improve their attitudes, improve their communication, and improve their skills, you can feel proud of the changes you've helped bring about. Wouldn't it be satisfying to know you have improved your team – just by improving yourself?

Continuous Improvement

Henry Kissinger served as National Security Advisor under U.S. presidents Richard Nixon and Gerald Ford. The story goes that his special assistant, Winston Lord, delivered a draft of a Presidential Foreign Policy Report to Kissinger one day. The next day, Kissinger called Lord into his office and asked, "Is this the best you can do?" Lord said he thought so, but he would give it another try. He revised the report and delivered the new draft to Mr. Kissinger.

The next morning, Kissinger called Lord into his office and asked again, "Is this the best you can do?" They repeated this process two more times, until Mr. Lord finally said, "I know this is the best I can do. I can't possibly improve one more word." Kissinger looked up at him and said, "In that case, now I'll read it."

This famous story is often used to illustrate the idea of continuous improvement. In the business world, continuous improvement often means eliminating waste and improving efficiency. This might be accomplished by reducing steps in a process or reducing resources. In the case of Mr. Kissinger and Mr. Lord, it meant improving a message by eliminating waste in language.

Continuous improvement means looking for ways to make things better. It begins with attitude. For continuous improvement to work, you and the members of your team have to have a desire to make things better – an attitude of helpfulness and willingness. But that's only the beginning. Once the attitude is in place, some kind of action needs to happen.

Oftentimes, the members of a team know what needs to change to make things better. They think about it and work out solutions in their minds. They talk to each other about it. They might even create a basic outline to get the change started. Then, someone says, "I don't know why we're talking about this. Around here, we always do it the way we've always done it."

In a situation like this, what can make a difference? Sometimes, all a team needs to break through negativity is the initiative of one person. Managers and business leaders are always looking for employees who can identify opportunities for improvement and take the lead to get it started. Your organization needs someone who's willing to take action! Could that person be you?

What steps might you take toward an improvement in your company? Here are some ideas:
- Talk to coworkers to see what they're thinking.
- Investigate the way things work now.

- Discuss with coworkers how things might be changed for the better.
- Take the idea to a manager – include an assessment of the problem, as well as any possible solutions.
- Offer to take responsibility for part of the implementation.

Continuous improvement isn't just about reducing steps in a process, increasing production, or tightening up the language in reports. It also involves the way people communicate and work cooperatively together. Can you think of better ways to communicate with your team? Maybe you identify additional sources of information to help with the project. If timelines aren't being met and people aren't being responsive, what could you do to make it better?

Continuous improvement is a philosophy that allows everyone to contribute ideas to make things better. It's not only allowed; it's a responsibility. Your ultimate goal is to help your organization reach its objectives. If you know of something that will help get there faster, or will help processes work better, your company leaders want to you to bring it up.

We will talk more about continuous improvement in the next chapter. It's a principle you can apply not only at work, but also in your personal life. That's what life is all about. Learning, growing, and getting better every day.

The Power to Make Things Better

Before you thought of yourself as a leader, you probably felt as though you were at the mercy of other people. You may have found yourself getting angry about things that didn't work. You might have judged others who were trying to fix problems. Can't they come up with better solutions? Why are they doing it that way? I'm tired of not getting what I need to do my job.

Now, you can see that getting angry and complaining do not make the situation better. In fact, this probably makes the situation worse. Now, when you see a problem anywhere in your organization that you can do something about, you know you have a responsibility to find a way to solve it. At the very least, it is your responsibility as an employee to tell someone when you see a problem, and then pitch in to fix it.

Better yet, what if you volunteered to lead a project team? Or you could offer to be a part of continuous improvement. As you go about your day, ask yourself, "What can I do to make this better?" With this attitude, you are no longer a victim of difficulties. You are taking action. You are acting as a leader.

Three Things to Remember

1. Projects always work better when the talents of the entire team are used to their fullest. Sharing responsibility is an important aspect of being an effective team member.

2. Leaders take initiative, pull resources together, and encourage their colleagues to stay organized and focused on the goal.

3. Your organization needs someone who's willing to take action! Could that person be you?

Putting it to Work

- Write down three valuable ideas from the chapter.

- What one thing can you do to start implementing each idea?

- What impact will taking action have on you or the team you lead?

Chapter 6
Making Things Better

Big Changes Are Coming

Movie stars have agents to help them find jobs. The agents guide their actor-actress customers through the process of finding the next script, auditioning for openings, and negotiating price. They watch for problems and fix them before their clients are too greatly affected, if possible. They stand by as advocates, looking out for the best interests of the stars, helping them navigate the sometimes choppy waters of the profession. The job of a Hollywood agent is to make things run as smoothly as possible.

In a similar way, employees sometimes act as change agents for their colleagues and their companies. This kind of agent watches for change and represents the interests of others. A change agent's job is to take care of business. To make sure everything runs smoothly. As the landscape of a business changes and shifts, a change agent stands by to facilitate the change. To help everyone in the organization navigate the sometimes choppy waters of business.

Have you ever been in this position? When things are changing in your organization, how do you respond? Do you watch for issues and take care of business, even as the routine is shifting around you? Can people count on you to make sure things run smoothly? If you have ever served in that role, you were being a change agent. The people you were helping weren't famous movie stars, but the change going on around them was probably just as challenging, in its way, as a movie star's high-stakes career.

Some people love change. Others hate it. In a company, some employees welcome change. Others fear it.

Lydia is the kind of person who loves change. If things stay the same too long, she gets bored. She becomes unmotivated and has even considered leaving the company. She sees things that need to change, and feels frustrated when nothing happens. When the changes come, she is relieved. "Finally!" she says. "Why did it take so long? It's about time some things changed around here." Now, when she comes to work in the morning, she is energized and eager to get started on the day.

Preston is the opposite of Lydia. He feels secure in the company's routine. The longer things stay the same, the calmer he feels. He sees things that could change, too, but he is afraid of upsetting the apple cart, so he doesn't say anything. When the changes come, he just closes his eyes and hopes it will go away. "I wish things would go back to the way they were," he thinks to himself. He knows he's supposed to jump in and go with the flow, but he just feels afraid and unsure of the future.

Consider all of the changes you've been involved with in the past 12 months. Even if you haven't been directly involved, what changes has your company gone through? Have you seen things shifting and changing in another department? Chances are you will be able to think of many changes that have been happening around you. Life is like that. Something is always changing!

Changes in the workplace can be the result of many things: new ideas, new technology, new buildings, innovation, increased knowledge, communication from new sources. What else?

Some changes are huge, such as changing to a new corporate software. Mergers and acquisitions can completely change an organization. Other changes are small, such as moving a workstation or painting a wall a different color. Large or small, change is change–and not always easy to manage.

When a company is reorganized or something else happens that affects the entire organization, you begin to see the effects of change on groups of people. While an organization is transitioning through massive changes, it's common for people within the company to deal with the changes in two distinct ways.

The first group concentrates on the new ideas change brings.
They look for new ways to make things more efficient and more effective. The people in this group are curious and learn from every person they meet throughout the change. They soak in the new experiences they are exposed to. They might do extra research and attend training sessions to help themselves and the organization. They volunteer to be on committees to aid the changes.

The second group feels unsettled by the new ideas change brings.
People in this group may appear to resistant new ideas, new information, and new processes. The reality is that many need time to process. Processing is demonstrated in multiple ways like saying nothing; simply thinking and researching. Some will talk to others about the changes, saying things like, "This doesn't make sense to me." They feel a great deal of stress through the

changes, and secretly, they may hope the changes don't actually happen.

Think about a big change that happened where you work. How did people react? Can you think of people who specifically fell into one of these two groups? Who embraced change and who resisted it? Which group did you fall into? Dealing with change begins with understanding how you feel about it. How would others describe your personal approach to change?

Change Is Here To Stay

Change requires a great deal of creativity and energy. To be successful, the entire team must pull together. When people resist change, they drag their feet and the energy level drops. They don't want to face change until they have to. Their resistance can drag others down, too. They might put off planning and organizing. They may decline opportunities to learn. As a result, the resisters of change can find themselves unprepared when the changes come. Some people convince themselves that changes will eventually cease. They might even look for ways to stop change, but that would be a battle that can't be won.

The thoughts and actions of those who resist can make everything a lot more difficult. Stalling for time and pushing against change can have a negative impact – on customers, coworkers, and the company.

Once you understand how you react to change yourself, you can use it to help others. If you are energized by change, you can share some of that energy with your colleagues. How can you use your influence to inspire them? What can you do to reassure them? If you are naturally resistant to change, you still can be a change agent. In some ways, you can be even more effective. Your colleagues will feel you understand what they're going through. You can help guide them to a more positive view of change.

It's true some things about change are difficult. But change truly can have a positive impact on an organization and the individuals in it. In the end, change is good. Think about why change happens in the first place. It usually means there is a better way. Someone may have noticed a new opportunity that could lead to more business. Perhaps an old way of doing things isn't working anymore. That old software is becoming obsolete, and no one is selling the way your company sells anymore.

Often, the leaders of a company have knowledge that leads them to make a change. Maybe the market is expanding and internal changes are necessary to survive. Perhaps there is an exciting opportunity to grow. Sometimes new regulations force companies to change. The good news is that leaders of most companies can see changes coming and take action to ensure the well-being of the organization and everyone in it.

Challenging the Status Quo

Being a change agent means making sure things run smoothly. Ironically, it also means challenging the status quo – shaking things up. It's been said the greatest obstacle to the growth and progression of a company is "The way we've always done it."

Change makes things better by improving on the status quo. By definition, change is a disruption. It necessarily alters our habits. We all have habits. Habits come from doing things over and over again, until we don't have to think about doing them. Our actions become automatic. Habits create efficiency, because we don't have to think about them. The research has already been done. The steps have already been planned. The bugs have already been worked out.

Imagine yourself driving home from work one day. As you drive, you go over everything you did at work in your mind. Then you think about the things you have yet to do that evening. Suddenly, you realize you're home and you can't remember how you got there! The streets you drive, the turns you make, the intersections you pass are so routine, they have become habit. You didn't have to think consciously about driving.

Habits are good for many things – habits such as taking medication, tying our shoes, or typing are good. You really don't have to think about how you do it. The habit makes it easier. On the other hand, some habits are not helpful. Consider how you react when you see someone cut you off in traffic or the response you have when you see an email from a person you don't particularly like. An angry or disgusted reaction could be a matter of habit, rather than a conscious choice. But is your habitual response to these events really necessary? Is it fair?

When big changes are happening at work, both good and bad habits are being disrupted. A disruption of good habits can present a challenge. You will have to find a new way to do things. A disruption of bad habits presents an opportunity. Challenging the status quo makes a space for improving things about yourself, your team, or your company.

Effective leaders and team members are conscious of what happens when habits are challenged. As they look for ways to make things better, they analyze how a change of habits might present challenges or opportunities. Good leaders don't change things for the sake of change. They find ways to improve overall results. Their ability to do this makes them valuable to the team, to their internal or external customers, and to the company. Change agents aren't afraid of disrupting the status quo, and they plan for the best ways to handle it. They are constantly asking,

"How can this be better?" and "what do we need to do to make it happen?"

Habits are not only physical or logistic actions. Habits can be thoughts, because thinking is an activity. If you think of things in the same way repeatedly, it becomes a habit of thought. Habitual thoughts include opinions.

We naturally and unconsciously form opinions about people, other departments and clients. Sometimes our opinion is positive, and sometimes it's negative. If you haven't really thought about it, your opinion may or may not be warranted. Have you ever stopped to validate your opinion? Ask yourself if you have evidence to back up your habit of thought. What if you took a different approach? It's always possible to gather more information and consider a different perspective on that person or group. New information could change your opinion.

Leon's job involves purchasing equipment for his company. Before he can select new machines, he has to work with the quality assurance department to build a set of criteria. He doesn't like collaborating with the QA group. They seem a little uppity to him. They always speak so adamantly about what is and isn't okay. Leon believes they like to throw their weight around. The truth is, he doesn't really know them that well. He's been working on making sure his opinions are backed up with facts. So, this time, he asks lots of questions to understand where the QA recommendations are coming from.

Leon discovers that Louise in QA has an extensive background in engineering and federal regulations. He didn't know that before! Instead of simply getting the information and leaving the QA office as quickly as he can (the way he used to do it), he sticks around for a while and learns more about how she earned her qualifications. When he asks about the equipment, she is happy to take a little extra time to explain why the criteria are so important. As a result, Leon is able to make more informed decisions about the equipment he brings to the table for the company's consideration.

Just as companies must look for constructive ways to change the status quo, so must individuals. Sometimes, it's just a matter of slowing down, analyzing the situation, gathering more information and making an informed choice. Don't be afraid to rock the boat, if there's a good reason!

Your Perspective

When we develop an opinion about something, sometimes we believe it's the only truth. After all, we've taken the time to gather the information and analyze it to back up our opinion. We believe we have more than enough evidence to prove our position. Many times, we forget our perspective is only one perspective. There are a variety of ways to look at any situation.

Parable of the Blind Man and the Elephant

A king asked six blind men to feel an elephant's body and tell him what an elephant is like. One blind man felt the elephant's leg and said an elephant is like a pillar. The blind man who felt the tail said an elephant is like a rope. The third blind man said the elephant is like a tree branch as he felt the elephant's trunk. One of the blind man felt an ear and said an elephant is like a hand fan. The fifth blind man, who felt the belly of the elephant, said the animal is like a wall. And the last of the six blind men said an elephant is like a solid pipe, because he felt a tusk.

The six blind men realized each of them was describing the elephant differently. How could that be? The King explained to them: All of you are right. Each of you is describing the elephant differently, because each of you touched a different part of the elephant's body. The elephant has all the features you mentioned.

As the parable explains, perspective is in the eye of the beholder. Two people can experience the same situation or hear the same information, and have two different perspectives or opinions. People are influenced by past events, habits of thought, their upbringings, and even recent conversations. Most people make judgments based on only the part of a story they see.

Next time you disagree with a coworker, stop and think. Consider your different perspectives. Why did things happen the way they did? How is your coworker's background different from yours? Try to think of reasons for her opinion. Did she come up through the company in a different department than you did? Does she come from a different cultural background? Think about the way she has approached other projects. You may find clues to the problem in her past decisions and behaviors.

Very often, it's not possible to guess. If you can't identify all the possible perspectives, this is the time to ask questions. Ask the other person to explain the reason for her opinion. Ask her to walk you through her perspective, sharing details to help you understand. Respectfully share your reasoning and details about your background as well. Take turns talking about the situation, with the idea that you're investigating this issue together. This is how people create a common understanding. It is also a great way to strengthen the bonds between you and your coworkers. Creating a common understanding helps reduce the tension caused by change. Best of all, it builds trust.

Decisions, Decisions

Every day, you make hundreds of decisions. You decide what time to get out of bed, when to leave for work, and what to get at the grocery store on the way home. At work, you decide how to go about completing a new project, who to ask for expertise, and when to take breaks (if you have that power). Some decisions are easy, while others are much more difficult.

Each decision you make has an impact on others around you. Even small decisions create ripples into other departments and other project teams. Sometimes, the decisions you make cause problems for your customers. Have you thought about how your decisions impact the rest of the company? Decision-making is very much a cause-and-effect exercise.

Let's take a look at one small example. When you receive email, how long would you wait to respond? Some people make it a habit to respond as soon as possible. Others don't want to train people to think they'll come running. So, they make it a point to wait 24 hours before replying. Waiting this long will have consequences. A delayed answer could prevent someone from doing their job. It could force a colleague to make a decision without your information.

In some cases, this kind of delay isn't a big deal. In other cases, such a delay could make a huge impact on whether a customer continues to do business with your company. Maybe your coworker simply needs some encouragement. If you take a few minutes to commend him for his work, it might be just what he needs to build his confidence.

Sometimes you don't have the authority to make the decisions you want to make. Think about where your authority begins and where it ends. In your position, do you have the authority to decide how to respond to a customer's email? To change project deadlines? To approach a person in another department to clarify a misunderstanding?

Odds are that you haven't really thought through these issues before, but it's important to understand where your authority comes from. Talk with your manager to make sure you've got it right–and don't forget that things change. Every now and then, check in with him and see if the lines of your authority still stand. They might even have expanded.

Many times, people don't believe they have the authority to take action or make decisions, but they really do. Once you understand the boundaries of your authority, it will make more sense to think about the impact of your decisions.

These two concerns work hand-in-hand. When you have the authority, you can make the decisions. You make decisions based on the authority you've been given. Is there a reason you haven't made decisions for which you have the authority? You may find you simply have a bad habit of not using the authority you have. Maybe you're afraid you'll make a mistake.

Have patience with yourself. The more you practice decision-making skills, the better you will get at making good decisions. As you gain experience with decision-making, your authority will tend to increase, and you'll find yourself making increasingly important decisions. You might need to point out to your boss that your decision-making abilities have improved substantially, and it's probably time to give you more responsibility – more authority. Don't give in to the habit of not making decisions. As your skills change, embrace the opportunity for more authority.

When your company faces big changes, don't be afraid to rock the boat. Don't hesitate to challenge the status quo, if that is what's called for. Use the skills you are learning in this book. Use your authority. Make those decisions! First and foremost, approach every decision with the intent of making things better for the company.

Problem-Solving Wisdom

Once you give yourself permission to make decisions and use your authority, it's time to think about specific problems you face. Big changes in a company create many challenges.

However, even when things are status quo, every day has its challenges. Effective leaders study the process of problem-solving and continually improve their skills.

Becoming a problem-solver is valuable to your organization. It helps your work groups, too. It's also a skill you can apply to assist your colleagues. Being a problem-solver is one of the qualities that makes you a leader – even if you don't have the title. Problem-solving removes barriers and allows things to move forward. When problems are solved, it reduces stress. It opens the way for creativity and brings people together.

Some problems are simple. How do you keep an office door from banging shut? You could install a hydraulic door closer. Or you could take the door off. How do you gain more desktop space? You could use stacking trays to clear space. Or you could add space with a rolling cart. These problems cause very little stress, and can even be fun to solve.

Some problems are more complex, or there's more at stake. What can your team do about conflicting schedules? Do you need to replace a team member, or can you make a compromise on the overlapping times?

How do you recommend a solution without alienating one coworker or the other? What if you're going to miss an important deadline that could cause the loss of the client? (You can feel a sense of dread just thinking about it, can't you?) Complex and high-stakes problems cause much more stress. They can be difficult to solve, but think of the sense of satisfaction when you do come up with a solution!

Sometimes your ability to solve the problem is a matter of mood or the ease with which your brain is working that day. Even a complex problem can be easy to solve on a day when your creative juices are flowing. Other times, even a simple problem can take forever to find a solution for. You may think for hours, but nothing comes to you. You get stuck.

People approach the situation in many different ways. Some simply do nothing, secretly hoping someone else will solve the problem. Others take it as a challenge. They keep thinking about possible solutions, even if it means stewing on the issue for days or weeks.

One of the best ways to solve problems is to get others involved. Putting your heads together will help you solve the problem. There are other benefits too. Other people's ideas may change your perspective, challenge your habits of thought, or get you out of a rut. Listening to other people's ideas gives you an opportunity to learn. It may help you better understand the potential impact of your decisions on other areas of the company.

Are you comfortable asking others for help? If you are feeling shy, remember people like to help. Working together on a problem builds trust between people. Remember to listen carefully to the ideas of other people and respond to show your respect and appreciation. Collaboration on problems also helps you learn more about each other. You might learn that Tamra is motivated by encouragement, whereas George works harder when somebody dares him to.

How does a person improve his or her problem-solving skills? You'll find many great materials about this to read. The best way may be to ask your manager or a mentor within your organization. Formal courses on problem-solving introduce you to classic theories that have been proven over time.

Promoting Your Idea

So, you've come up with a great solution to a project-related problem. And you want to suggest a way to improve your department's workflow. Good for you! You're using all those new skills you've learned. At your level of authority, you probably can implement that project-related problem. However, you may not have the authority to modify your department's processes. You'll have to go through channels to get that idea approved.

First, identify the person you need to approach for approval. Your manager can help you figure it out, if you don't know. If this person agrees with your idea, approval will be easy. But what if the person doesn't agree? How can you increase your chances of gaining their support?

Idea Presentation Tips:
1. **Choose a strategic time to make suggestions and share ideas.** Don't pick a time when your boss is stressed, frustrated, or trying to multi-task. Schedule a meeting time that makes sense for both you and your manager. Make sure it's a time when he can give you his full attention.

2. **Have a plan.** Research your idea, write an agenda for the meeting, and come prepared with background information. Before you try to make a presentation, make sure you fully understand the potential impact of your suggestion. How will it affect other departments? How could it affect your service or product? How might it affect your efficiency and quality?

3. **Make sure you've thought about your idea from different perspectives.** Ask other coworkers about their

thoughts. Present the idea informally to your team, and ask them to help you weigh all possibilities. Are any pieces missing? Who could you speak with to make sure you fill all the gaps?

4. **Speak your manager's language.** Before you present a new idea, you need to know your manager's priorities and goals. What language does he use to talk about his goals? Use the same language in your presentation. This will help him understand what you are saying. Familiar language will help him make a connection with your idea and visualize how it could help achieve his priority or goal. If your manager is budget conscious, communicate how your suggestion will impact cost.

5. **Ask questions.** Don't assume you have the whole story. Your manager might know things you don't know. Ask questions to find out more. How does the process work? What's the ultimate outcome we hope to reach? Take responsibility for understanding everything you can about the way your idea will impact the company, your department, your manager, and your coworkers. Don't forget about customers! Does your manager have a different perspective than you? Ask intelligent questions to figure out why, and see if your idea still fits. At the very least, your manager will appreciate your initiative.

6. **Control your emotions.** Before you present your idea, take a moment to imagine how it might go. What could go wrong? In your mind, go over every possible response from your manager. How will you reply? Some of his answers could make you feel angry or frustrated. Prepare

yourself for these feelings, and think ahead of time about how you would like to respond. How can you remain professional? Becoming defensive or aggressive won't help your cause. Stay level-headed. Be open to hearing your manager's ideas, as well sharing your own.

7. **Share your idea more than once.** Sometimes a person needs to hear an idea more than one time before it really resonates. Don't give up. Make a note of the things you learned when you asked questions. Store the information where you can find it later. When the time is right for a future conversation, adjust your idea or suggestion and bring it up again.

Sometimes it takes a while to receive approval on a new idea. At first, you may think you're being ignored. Or you may jump to conclusions if you haven't heard an answer and think the answer is no. It can be difficult to have patience.

Try to remember, no news is sometimes good news. Maybe more than one person needs to approve your idea. It takes time to consider logistics and determine the extent of any impact on others. Maybe your idea is being vetted. Or this might be one of those times when something is going on you aren't aware of. It doesn't mean your idea is not a good one. Keep asking questions, making suggestions, and checking in with your manager. You'd be surprised what a little communication can do!

Looking Ahead to the Future

It's hard to know where you might be in the future and what you might be doing. Maybe you have a clear idea of where you would like to go. Or maybe you just know you would like to keep progressing in your career. It would be satisfying to use the skills you've learned in this course to become more involved in your organization and continue growing and learning.

In a way, it doesn't matter where you'll be or what you will be doing in the future. You can be a leader or effective team member anywhere! Through the work you've done in this book, you now know more than you did before about things like communicating effectively, influencing others, managing time and projects, navigating difficult conversations, and taking initiative. All are skills that fit many different situations. Remember, leaders and effective team members influence people and organizations and manage projects in many different venues from families, clubs, and charities to schools and places of work.

The more you use what you've learned in this book, the more skilled you'll become. It will get easier and more comfortable, too. Throughout this book, you've been thinking a lot about what it takes to be a leader. We've spent a great deal of time carefully analyzing what makes people and companies successful. But going forward, with practice, these abilities will become second nature.

In what ways do you believe these lessons will make a difference for you? What happens when a person learns to communicate clearly, have a great attitude, collaborate effectively, and lead responsibly? If you tackle any goal using these abilities, you can hardly keep from succeeding! Naturally, you will face many kinds of challenges, and no one can promise easy success. But the tools you have now give you a better chance of moving forward into a life and work you have visualized for yourself.

This book may be coming to a close, but your opportunities for learning will never end. Think of all the new opportunities you can unlock for yourself through continuous improvement.

Imagine the respect and admiration you'll now have a chance to earn from your colleagues and managers. You can become one of the people in your organization who is counted on to solve problems, move things forward, and bring people and resources together to accomplish goals. That's something you can be proud of!

Three Things to Remember

1. Change requires a great deal of creativity and energy. To be successful, the entire team must pull together.

2. Have you ever stopped to validate your opinion? Ask yourself if you have evidence to back up your habit of thought.

3. Many times, people don't believe they have the authority to take action or make decisions, but they really do.

Putting it to Work

- Write down three valuable ideas from the chapter.

- What one thing can you do to start implementing each idea?

- What impact will taking action have on you or the team you lead?

About Revela

We Know Leadership.
And we know how to get results.

Revela (Rah-vel-a): to reveal, make known, discover, or divulge.

It's an experience. An exploration of untapped skills, hidden qualities that can be molded and transformed into a leadership style that engages employees, creates excitement, garners respect, and leads to greater outcomes for the organization.

Revela is an organization specializing in the development of leaders in all levels of the organization. Based in Omaha, Nebraska, Revela is one of the region's most experienced thought challengers, helping individuals and companies across the country unleash their potential.

Revela's passion is fueled by positive experiences and individual growth. With a belief in relationships, community, supporting others, and delivering business results, Revela goes beyond the expected to benefit the collective cause. Fully authentic and down to earth, Revela's confidence and pride stems from the positive change in others.

Founded in 1989, Revela believes in the untapped human potential, that everyone has value, and that fundamentally everyone deserves a chance at success. Taking a different approach to development because they see things differently, the Revela team goes beyond the expected to help individuals discover their strengths, transform their weaknesses, and experience an even greater level of professional and personal growth. For more information about Revela, visit RevelaGroup.com or call 712.322.1112.

Your leaders. Our passion.

1508 Leavenworth Street
Omaha, NE 68102

Email: info@RevelaGroup.com
Call: (712) 322-1112
Visit: www.RevelaGroup.com

References

Amabile, T.M., et al (1977). "Social roles, social control, and biases in social-perception processes." *Journal of Personality and Social Psychology, vol* 35, pp 485-494.

Armour, R. (1971). *Writing light verse and prose humor.* The Writer, Inc., Boston, MA.

Blubaugh, D. (1965). "The Blind Men and the Elephant." World Wise Schools. Retrieved from http://www.peacecorps.gov/wws/stories/blind-men-and-elephant/

CFI Group (2012). *CFI Contact Center Satisfaction Index.* Retrieved from http://www.cfigroup.com/downloads/CCSI_2012.pdf

Cline-Thomas & Chang (2016). "Elementary School Accidentally Sends 'Hurt Feelings Report' to Parents." NBC Universal Media. Retrieved from http://www.nbcphiladelphia.com/news/local/Hurt-Feelings-Report-Lombardy-Elementary-School-Brandywine-School-District-Email-Delaware-369189861.html

Covey, S. (2013). *The 7 Habits of Highly Effective People: Powerful Lessons in Personal Change.* Simon and Schuster, Inc., New York, NY.

Dictionary.com (2016). "Definition of Facilitate." Dictionary.com. Retrieved from http://www.dictionary.com/browse/facilitate

Doran, G., et al. (1981). "There's a S.M.A.R.T. way to write management's goals and objectives." *Management Review (vol. 70, issue 11).*

Eastman, H. (2013). "Communication Changes with Technology, Social Media." *The Daily Universe.* Retrieved from http://universe.byu.edu/2013/07/07/1communication-changes-with-technology-social-media/

Einstein, A. (n.d.) Quote. Retrieved from http://www.goodreads.com/quotes/60780-if-i-had-an-hour-to-solve-a-problem-i-d

Gaston, P. M. (1808), *Maximes et réflexions sur différents sujets de morale et de politique.* Maxim xvii, Paris, France.

Gilbert, D. & Malone, P. (1995). "The correspondence bias." *Psychological Bulletin, vol 117,* pp 21-38.

Ivanov, M., et al (2010). "Behavioral communication: Individual differences in communication style." *Personality and Individual Differences, Vol. 49.* Retrieved from

http://www.sciencedirect.com/science/article/pii/S01918869
10001017

Joybell, C. (n.d.) Quote. Retrieved from http://www.goodreads.com/quotes/424700-we-can-t-be-afraid-of-change-you-may-feel-very

Killman, T. (1974). *Thomas-Killman Conflict Mode Instrument.* Retrieved from http://www.kilmanndiagnostics.com/catalog/thomas-kilmann-conflict-mode-instrument

Loder, V. (2014). "Five Best To-Do List Tips." *Forbes Magazine online.* Retrieved from http://www.forbes.com/sites/vanessaloder/2014/06/02/five-best-to-do-list-tips/#552845351b53

Luft, J. & Ingham, H. (1955). "The Johari window, a graphic model of interpersonal awareness." *Proceedings of the western training laboratory in group development.* University of California, Los Angeles, CA.

McCormack, M. (1984). *What They Don't Teach You at Harvard Business School.* Bantam Books, New York, NY.

McGonigal, J. (n.d.). Quote. Retrieved from http://www.brainyquote.com/quotes/quotes/j/janemcgoni560550.html

Mehrabian, A. (1972). *Silent Messages: Implicit Communication of Emotions and Attitudes.* Wadsworth Publishing Company, Belmont, CA.

Merriam-Webster (2015). "Definition of Influence." *Merriam-Webster Online Dictionary.* Retrieved from http://www.merriam-webster.com/dictionary/influence

Merriam-Webster (2015). "Definition of Intention." *Merriam-Webster Online Dictionary.* Retrieved from http://www.merriam-webster.com/dictionary/intention

Meyer, P., et al (2014). *Effective Leadership Development.* The Meyer Resource Group, Inc., Waco, TX.

National Security Agency (n.d.). "Mokusatsu: One Word, Two Lessons." *NSA.Gov.* Retrieved from https://www.nsa.gov/news-features/declassified-documents/cryptologic-spectrum/assets/files/mokusatsu.pdf

Reagan, R. & Weatherford, J. (2013). "Is This the Best We Can Do?" *Government Finance Review,* Government Finance Officers Association.

Sage Software Survey (2007). "Time Management Statistics." Key Organization Systems. Retrieved from http://www.keyorganization.com/time-management-statistics.php

Saint-Exupery, A. (1995). *The Little Prince.* Wordsworth Editions Limited, Hertfordshire, UK.

Twain, M. (1901). *A Connecticut Yankee in King Arthur's Court.* Harper & Brothers Publishers, NY.

Virginia DHRM (n.d.). "An Overview of Employee Dispute Resolutions." *Virginia Department of Human Resource Management.* Retrieved from http://www.dhrm.state.va.us/resources/conferencepresentations/AnOverviewofEmployeeDisputeResolutionsConflictResolutionServices4.pdf.

Vistage International (n.d.). Work on Your Business with CEOs, Executives and Owners. www.vistage.com

Wiley (2013). *Everything DiSC.* John Wiley & Sons, Inc.

www.ingramcontent.com/pod-product-compliance
Lightning Source LLC
Chambersburg PA
CBHW050005230526
45465CB00003BB/1268